SOLVING

SEPARATION

Anxiety

**Over 77
Savvy Solutions** *for*
**Herd-Bound
Behavior**

KATHY BAAR

for Raising The Baar, LLC

ABOUT KATHY BAAR

Kathy Baar is a 4-Star Parelli Senior Instructor and Horse Development Specialist currently located in Lexington, KY.

With over 25 years in the horse industry, and 18 years dedicated to the study of horse psychology, Kathy brings depth of knowledge and understanding to her students.

Her dedication to horses and to the humans that own them earned her a teaching position on the Parelli Faculty for over five years. In that role she was able to impact the lives of over 3,000 horsemanship students and help to raise the level of 'horse-man-ship' worldwide.

Kathy is passionate about helping others find the joy that originally drew them to horses, by overcoming the obstacles standing in their way.

When she isn't helping people achieve their goals with horses, Kathy enjoys hopping around the eventing course and spending time cultivating a love of nature with her son.

She is currently working to help jump riders and horses reach greater heights and become happier athletes by increasing their understanding of equine psychology.

You can reach Kathy at: contact@jkbaar.com.

Raising The Baar LLC
contact@jkbaar.com

For information regarding Workshops,
Programs or Products please contact Kathy Baar at:
contact@jkbaar.com.

*Horse activities can be dangerous. Do not attempt to use any of
these techniques or exercises without proper education and safety
equipment. Raising The Baar LLC and/or Kathy Baar and/or
Parelli Natural Horsemanship are not responsible for the improper
or unsafe use of these techniques.*

ISBN-13: 978-1537529950

ISBN-10: 1537529951

For John, Luke, and the Horse.

ACKNOWLEDGEMENTS

I would like to thank some of the people who have been an immeasurable help in the production of this book.

First, to my family, for listening to my rambling as I hashed out my ideas and thoughts on Separation Anxiety. Also, for helping me make the time to get those ideas into print. The process was not speedy and my family may not have been such enthusiastic supporters in the beginning had they known how large the project would be.

Thank you, John Baar, for the photographs, the time, the support and the advice. Without you this book would not be here.

Thank you to my friends who provided excellent suggestions and feedback on what helped them learn the most from educational guides. Also, thank you friends for your enthusiasm and positive energy.

Thank you to the outside support team that lent their suggestions and time. Without their expert opinions and advice I wouldn't have been able to get to this point.

Thank you to the Parelli Program for helping me discover the psychology of horses and helping me to understand their beautiful nature. This program taught me the importance of "Walking a minute or a mile in your horse's horse shoes."

Most importantly I would like to thank God for helping with the creating process. The time needed to create and publish this book was immense and on more than one occasion it was a true miracle that any progress was made!

Without those miracles I would not be typing these acknowledgements. Thank you God for the many and often unacknowledged daily miracles you provide!

– Kathy Baar

CONTENTS OVERVIEW

Acknowledgments ... *v*

Introduction ... *1*

Theory ... *7*

1. Horses Kept In The Pasture In A Herd ... *45*

16 specific exercises for horses kept in a herd

In addition you can use most of the exercises from horses "Kept In Pairs."

2. Horses Kept In A Stall Or Barn ... *85*

19 specific exercises for horses kept in the stall

In addition you can use most of the exercises from horses "Kept In Pairs."

3. Horses Kept In Pairs Or With A Buddy ... *129*

15 specific exercise for horses kept with a buddy

*Once your horse is confident outside of the pen,
all exercises from "Horses Kept In The Herd" can be
used with 'the buddy' in place of 'the herd.'*

4. Riding With A Buddy Horse/s ... *165*

13 Specific Exercises to help you while riding

5. Emergency Strategies & Exercises ... *197*

14 Specific Exercises to help you in the moment

6. Pattern Progress Pages ... *221*

CONTENTS

Theory Section

Horse Psychology 8

Horsenalities 10

Human Psychology. 13

How To Get Your Horse In The "Learning Zone" 16

Developing "Confidence Muscles" In Our Horses 20

Separation Anxiety Or A High Propensity For Bonding? . 24

Creating New Patterns. 28

Creating An Icon Of Safety. 29

A Note On Tying 30

Using Multiple Exercises In A Session 32

Catching Game And Creating Draw 33

Building Your Herd Of Two 35

Ending A Session 36

Me And My Shadow Game:
 Pre-Requisite To Getting Started 37

Horse's Body Language 42

How To Get Started. 44

Section 1

Horses Kept In The Pasture In A Herd ... *45*

16 specific exercises for horses kept in a herd

In addition you can use most of the exercises from horses "Kept In Pairs."

Horsenality Filter. 46

Helpful References:
Zones Of The Horse, The Seven Games. 48

Exercises

1. Yielding To And Fro 50
2. Zone 3 "Touch It" 52
3. Backwards Around The Herd's Bubble 54
4. "Stop Sign:" Backwards 56
5. Yielding The HQ Until You Get The Other Eye . 58
6. Yo-Yo Game 60
7. Transitions On The Circle 62
8. Zone 3 Mirror 64
9. 1 Million Transitions 66
10. Connection Through Circling Changes 68
11. Close Range Circling 70
12. Sideways Around Herd 72
13. Sideways From Porcupine 74
14. Over Or Between 76
15. Sideways And Squeeze Combo 78
16. Circling To Sideways 81

Section 2

Horses Kept In A Stall Or Barn ... *85*

19 specific exercises for horses kept in the stall

In addition you can use most of the exercises from horses "Kept In Pairs."

Horsenality Filter 86

Helpful References:
Zones Of The Horse, The Seven Games. 88

Exercises

17. Follow A Feel, You Choose The Zone 90

18. Circling In Stall 92

19. Sideways Point To Point In Stall. 94

20. Sideways Towards With Porcupine On The Rope . 96

21. Backwards Responsibility. 98

22. Yielding Sideways Away From Steady Pressure . . 100

23. "Touch It" 102

24. Approach And Retreat 104

25. Backwards Through And Out 106

26. Drive HQ/FQ, Then Drive From Zone 3 108

27. Touch It With Foot/Nose/Tail 110

28. Explore The Area From Zone 3 112

29. Close Range Circling And Zone 3 Driving 114

30. Sideways Point To Point In Aisle 116

31. Squeeze To Sideways Down Aisle 118

32. Squeeze Game In And Out Of Barn 120

33. Sideways Out Of Barn. 122

34. Spiral To The Grass 124

35. Driving From Zone 3 On A "Trail Ride" 126

Section 3

Horses Kept In Pairs Or With A Buddy ... *129*

15 specific exercise for horses kept with a buddy

Once your horse is confident outside of the pen,
all exercises from "Horses Kept In The Herd" can be used
with 'the buddy' in place of 'the herd.'

Horsenality Filter 130

Helpful References:
Zones Of The Horse, The Seven Games. 132

Exercises

    36. Friendly Game In Motion 134

    37. Extreme Friendly Game By Buddy 136

    38. Clipping By Buddy 138

    39. Vet Prep By Buddy. 140

    40. Farrier Prep By Buddy. 142

    41. Lead By Leg 144

    42. Backwards Circles 146

    43. Strengthening Your "Yo" 148

    44. Backwards Weave. 150

    45. Backwards 'S' 152

    46. Falling Leaf 154

    47. Figure 8 By Buddy 156

    48. Rock Slide. 158

    49. Jumps By Buddy 160

    50. Trailer Load By Buddy. 162

Section 4

Riding With A Buddy Horse/s ... *165*

13 Specific Exercises to help you while riding

Horsenality Filter 166
Helpful References:
Zones Of The Horse, The Seven Games. 167

Exercises

51. Sideways Dance. 169
52. HQ/FQ Ballet 172
53. Soft Touch Comfort Zone Stretch 174
54. Beep-Beep 176
55. Swing The Energy 178
56. Rock Weight Front To Back By Buddy 180
57. Lollipop 182
58. Backwards Circle 184
59. Circle Splits 186
60. Sideways Away 188
61. "Sideways Wars" 190
62. Rider Squeeze. 192
63. Pairs Dance 194

Section 5

Emergency Strategies & Exercises ... *197*

14 Specific Exercises to help you in the moment

Horsenality Filter 198

Emergency Strategies

64. Trailering Challenges 200

65. At The Clinic 201

66. My Horse Is Worried In The Stall 202

67. My Horse Is Scared In The Arena 203

68. My Horse Is Attached To The Horse
He Trailered In With 204

69. My Horse Is Attached To Someone
Or Something Still In The Barn 205

70. My Horse Has Druthers Towards His
Buddy/Food/Stall/People/Etc. 206

71. Challenges In Class While The Group Is Gathered . 207

Emergency Exercises

72. Use Your Buddy! 209

73. Scared Of The Arena Edges 211

74. Half Circles At The Wall On The Ground . . . 213

75. Box Step While Riding 215

76. To And Fro While Riding 217

77. Swaying In The "Breeze" While Riding 219

Section 6

Pattern Progress Pages ... *221*

INTRODUCTION

Why Did I Write This Partnership Guide?

As I travel the world one common theme that comes up is "horse bound" horses (sometimes referred to as "barn sour," "buddy sour," etc.). This problem creates all sorts of frustrating and dangerous scenarios.

After having a baby myself I had a realization about the trauma horses go through every day when separated from their herd or buddy. This can be much like weaning an infant from his mother! This may sound dramatic, but as we look at a horse's nature; the act of leaving the herd can be as frightening and traumatic for horses as the weaning process, or a human infant being separated from their mother.

For anyone who has ever been a parent or a mother, the thought of having someone take your baby can make you physically sick, but at least adult humans have the intellect to realize the baby will simply be in the other room getting a bath, or with grandma who needs some bonding time for a while.

However, the infant doesn't have this luxury. Life for a baby human is much like life for horses, in that they do not understand the words "we'll be right back," or "you'll be fine, we're only leaving for a moment."

1

Both babies and horses experience similar sensory panic when separated from everything they know to be safe and comfortable. It can not only be physiologically stressful but also has physical ramifications such as sweating, screaming, colic, etc.!

This BFO (Blinding Flash of the Obvious) helped me see the issue of "barn sour" (more correctly; "barn sweet" – more to come on why this problem is a barn 'sweet' problem, not barn 'sour') in a whole new light, and because of this I am able to present solutions for this 'problem' in a different way. A way that has made more lasting and more effective changes for students and the horses they love.

I would like to share the theory behind this approach and some specific exercises that can help your horse build a bond with you as the leader. I am passionate about this subject, and hope to shed some light on an approach to separating horses that can be non-stressful and constructive to your relationship with your horse.

What Will You Be Doing As You Work Your Way Through This Book?

This book is designed to give you specific exercises to set up a pattern for your horse of Safety and Comfort away from the herd. You will be building Confidence in your horse and allowing his responses to guide you in the speed of your progression.

Pat Parelli has given us the PRINCIPLES that will outline how we communicate with the horse.

Our PURPOSE is to create a confident partner in new environments, away from the equine herd.

The TIMElines will be set by how your horse responds.

When Do You Use This Book?

This guide is set up as a way to prepare for the future. You will need to build a pattern BEFORE the day you expect your horse to 'perform.' We will embrace the concept Pat Parelli has outlined: "Prior and Proper PREPARATION prevents P-poor performance;" while keeping in mind that most of the time *taking the time it takes now*, will save time in the future.

Where Do You Use This Book?

You can take the book with you to the barn so you are reminded of the exercises and goals, or you can read it at home and take the concepts with you, to your horse.

Another great tool is using the camera portion of your phone to take a picture of the exercise and directions for your day. This allows you to create your own "Pocket Guide."

In addition, the last section of the book contains work pages that I recommend you take to the barn. These are sheets for you to keep track of your "program" (the days you have practiced these concepts) with your horse.

How Do You Use This Book?

1. Read and re-read the theory section, this is the MOST important thing to understand. If you can understand and approach things from your horse's perspective it will entirely change your interactions with your horse!

   Also, I feel the Parelli method is the most useful and comprehensive method to developing horses and creating a language to "talk" with them. If you are unfamiliar with the Parelli approach you can go to: www.parelli.com to find out more. If you have questions about the Parelli Seven Games, the parelli.com website is the best place to get your answers.

2. Find the section that is most appropriate for how your horse is kept; Stall, Pasture with a Herd, or in a Pair with one other buddy horse.

3. At the beginning of each section you will find a Horsenality™ Filter, this will help you customize your session to exactly what your horse needs.

4. Begin by trying one of the exercises. At the beginning of each exercise you will find prerequisite information to help set you up for success. Follow the exercises and repeat them in a pattern to help grow your horse's ability to stay calm in situations away from the herd/barn/farm.

You will find Pattern Progress Pages at the end of the book to help you keep track of your sessions. Use this to track the days you play with these concepts.

5. Each section includes some troubleshooting tips, if you aren't making progress refer to these tips for help. Also, some sections include a "How to Advance," which gives you the option to complete the exercise at a higher level.

6. After you have completed the exercises best suited to your horse and you have developed his self-confidence, there is an additional section for some "Emergency Strategies."

These strategies will be useful when you find yourself in a situation away from home/out on the trail/at an event, and everything falls apart. Keep in mind this is not where to start! It is included to help give you some ideas on how to stay safe and get the most out of the situation when everything falls apart.

As an added note, you may find valuable information in each section of the book that you can utilize in current situations, or future situations with your horse.

No matter what the living circumstances are for your horse, most of the exercises in each section can be adjusted to fit you and your horse. I encourage you to look over the other sections, specifically the ground section that applies to your horse, the Riding section, and the Emergency Strategies in the last section.

Seven Games – Five Zones – Four Savvys

As Pat Parelli reminds us when playing with our horses, "There are only Seven Games, in five Zones, in Four Savvys: On Line *(groundwork with ropes of varying lengths)*, Liberty *(groundwork without any ropes)*, FreeStyle *(riding with loose reins and no contact)*, and Finesse *(riding with contact, performing precision manoeuvres)*.

This is the foundation of communication with our horses and *all you need to know to become excellent*. In addition, it can be helpful to see these games put into practice in real life scenarios and in imaginative combinations to help solve real life 'problems' (soon to be known as 'puzzles').

Throughout This Book I Will Do
Just That By Using

- 63 Preparation Exercises (exercises to be done in preparation and before you need your horse to "perform" for you, away from the herd).

- 8 "Emergency" Strategies, for in-the-moment Savvy Tips and reminders.

- 6 "Emergency" Exercises with specific steps to follow to

help your horse in the moment of trouble.

By completing the exercises throughout the book and incorporating the theory into your everyday interactions with your horse, you will be able to solve herd-bound issues by building a more powerful relationship with your horse – a relationship that your horse enjoys as much as you do.

"Prior and proper preparation prevents P-Poor Performance."—Pat Parelli

THEORY

*First, learn the WHY behind your horse's
herd-bound behavior.*

*Second, learn a relationship and pattern-based
approach to solving this issue.*

To solve the 'problem' of horses wanting to be with the herd or at the barn/stall we need to create a situation where our horses are 'happy' being with us and CHOOSE us over the herd/barn. In order to do this we need to understand the horse's perspective, our (human) natural tendencies, and how these natural tendencies can either erupt in chaos or grow into the ultimate partnership.

The more we understand BOTH unique perspectives of the horse-man-ship relationship, the better we can approach new puzzles (previously viewed as problems) with our horses, and the more effective we can become as leaders.

To shine a light on these perspectives the following pages talk briefly about:

- **The Nature Of Horses**
  Horse Psychology and Horsenalities: These topics will help you understand where your horse is coming from.

- **The Nature Of Humans**
  Human Psychology and Separation Anxiety: To help you understand why a human's normal approach is so different to what horses understand.

- **Building A Better Partner**
  How To Get Your Horse In The Learning Zone, Developing 'Confidence Muscles' In Our Horses, Creating New Patterns, Creating An Icon Of Safety, A Note on Tying and Catching Game/Creating Draw. These topics will help you develop a more willing and confident partner with increased calmness away from the herd.

- **Developing A Good Session**
  Using Multiple Exercises In A Session, Building Your Herd Of Two, Me And My Shadow, Horse's Body Language, and Ending a Session. All of this information is given to help you build the most effective and efficient session with your horse.

- **How To Get Started**
  With all your new understanding about Herd-Bound Behavior and solutions to set you up for success, this step-by-step guide will help you get started.

Horse Psychology

Horses are prey animals; their very survival depends on staying with the herd. Their DNA is designed in a way to encourage them to stay with the group, and their underlying philosophy is safety in numbers!

By asking a horse to leave the herd and come with us (a predator) we have to first understand that we are asking them to overwrite everything that years of nature has *programmed* them to do. We are asking them to go against their instinct; to do something that could and would naturally get them killed.

To survive, horses must be in-the-moment thinkers; they can learn from their past but they don't get stuck living in it. What this means to us is that even if we had a great one hour session with our horse last week, he has spent the last 168 hours (1 week) finding comfort, safety, food and play (his hierarchy of needs) with his herd. In effect, he has re-programmed himself to get everything he needs, with the herd. Understanding this helps us understand why it can feel as if we are "starting over" again each session/week/month.

What Are We Asking Our Horses To Do By Leaving The Herd?

We are asking them to compromise not only their comfort but also their perception of safety. There is only one other situation in the equine life that is similar, and that is when horses are weaned from their mother. This can be done in a gradual, supportive and confidence-building scenario; where the horse never realizes they need to be fearful. Or it can be done in a traumatic and abrupt style that decreases self-confidence and increases stress, fear, and distrust.

In this book we will embrace a style of 'weaning' our horses from the herd that will increase their self-confidence as well as increase their trust in us as the leader.

Each time we set a goal of getting our horses less herd-bound it is vital that we create a pattern to achieve success. The process can only succeed if we approach it from a gradual and progressive mindset.

Separation Anxiety is not something that has a one-time fix. In fact, using a one-time fix mindset can often cause the separation anxiety to become more magnified.

Pat Parelli says horses are like computers, "they rarely do what we want, but they always do what they are programmed to do." In this book we will look at patterns to help you 're-program' your horse to find comfort and relaxation away from the herd, and with you.

Horsenalities

Understanding your horse's Horsenality can be a powerful tool to progressing. It can help you respond more appropriately, with a more specific strategy to help your horse make the most effective change. However, a comprehensive knowledge of Horsenalities is not a pre-requisite to having success in this Separation Anxiety guide.

There are Horsenality charts at the beginning of each section to provide a more specific filter for you and your horse. Some of these charts also include recommendations for the exercises you may find most effective for your horse.

On the flip side, if you are unsure of your horse's Horsenality, or he often switches between two or more Horsenalities, feel free to progress through each exercise adjusting as you need.

The important thing to keep in mind is; horses have four primary needs (other than breeding); Safety, Comfort, Play and Food. If you are able to meet these needs for your horse and be seen as the provider of these needs you will start to develop a more meaningful relationship with your horse. As you build this relationship he will begin to seek you out and choose to spend time with you rather than trying to get away from you.

With this approach we will talk about establishing patterns that create draw towards you and away from the herd. One of the most powerful tools we can use when training horses is to create motivation: if our horses are motivated to be with us the issue of 'barn sour' becomes void.

Once you realize the power of 'draw' in motivating horses, it is easy to understand why Pat Parelli uses the term "BARN SWEET" rather than "Barn Sour" because, in fact, horses love the barn and want to get back there as soon as possible. In the horse's mind everything about the barn is

SWEET, not sour.

The new goal is to create a horse that is "Human Sweet" so that your horse can't wait to be with you and doesn't want to leave!

The following chart gives some general words and descriptions for each Horsenality. The pictures give a quick impression of how each Horsenality type may appear physically when observing or playing with that horse.

Left-Brain EXTROVERT	Right-Brain EXTROVERT
Left-Brain INTROVERT	Right-Brain INTROVERT

The Parelli Horsenality™ Chart

Right-Brain Extrovert

This horse constantly needs reassurance. He gets confused easily and then gets afraid, so he needs you to make things simple, which will help him relax.

Right-Brain Introvert

This shy, timid, shrinking violet avoids pressure by retreating into himself. Success involves going very slowly at first and waiting for him to come out of his shell, to trust more. Pretty soon he'll be offering you more.

Left-Brain Introvert

Welcome to the land of "Why should I? What's in it for me?" This horse reads people like a book. He knows what you want and he's not going to give it to you, unless you treat him right. Even though he appears stubborn or lazy, he's not at all lazy in the mind! He may move slowly, but he's always thinking quickly.

Left-Brain Extrovert

This horse is a playful character that needs interesting things to do. He is obsessed with learning and needs variety and new things to keep it fun.

By applying the Horsenality filter to your horse appropriately you will be able to more quickly help your horse make the changes you desire. When you address his Horsenality specifically it gives him what he needs sooner so he is able to make a faster change.

For exercises that will most specifically 'speak' to each Horsenality you can refer to the charts at the beginning of each section; Page 46 for 'Horses Kept In A Herd,' page 86 for 'Horses Kept In A Stall,' and page 130 for 'Horses Kept In Pairs.'

Human Psychology

By nature, humans are direct line and goal oriented, we come up with a goal and move directly towards it until we achieve the goal. For example; we decide to go on a relaxing trail ride with our horsey friends. Next we head to the pasture with our halter in hand and often find our horse difficult to catch. We corner them anyway, saddle up and get on.

During this process our horse may be whinnying to the herd and pulling on the lead to turn around. However, "we are at the barn to go on a trail ride..." So, off we go and about half-way down the trail our dream has turned into our nightmare (not to mention how the horse is feeling about the situation), and we give up because our "stupid horse" is clearly too neurotic to be a trail horse! It is this ability to be goal driven that helps us achieve great things, but it is also what gets us in trouble with our horses.

Humans also tend to think about the past or the future – we have trouble staying present and in the moment. Often, rather than seeing the horse that is in front of us today, we are thinking about what he did to us last week, or the champion he could be next year (if he would only quit screaming and dragging us back to the barn)!

When we think about the past and future rather than the moment, this keeps us from 'reading' our horses and from seeing what they actually need. Pat has a brilliant saying; "Do your thinking at night and your feeling during the day." This is a valuable lesson to learn and embrace while playing with horses. It can help your feel and timing – two essential keys to success!

In addition, humans are almost always thinking about what OTHER people are thinking about them. Humans can be so preoccupied with what others might be thinking that they are unaware of what they, themselves, are thinking and even less aware of what the horse is thinking.

When horses and humans keep thinking like they are programmed to, they cannot act like partners. Some of the effects are;

• Horses get more fearful of predatory behavior, they may become hard to catch, pull away, become unpredictable and hard to manage.

  Personal Story: I have a vivid memory of what this looks like. Before I learned how to become my horse's partner I owned a horse who had very little desire to be with me. In fact, in order to catch her I had to bring 13 other mares in out of her field (that was EVERY horse in the paddock), put them in their stalls, and then I had a chance of "tricking" my horse into being caught. At which point I had to put her in her stall so that I could turn the other 13 mares back out! I was so unaware that things could be different that I viewed this scenario as "normal" horse behavior and an average day!

• Sometimes horses can become more dominant, kicking, biting and doing everything but what you ask.

• Often, humans get scared and hurt, giving up on their dreams and selling their horses.

- Occasionally humans get frustrated and mad, they become unfair and sometimes cruel to the horses when they run out of knowledge.

HOWEVER

When horses and humans come together, BEAUTIFUL things can be achieved; they can form an unbreakable team!

When this happens the result is a pleasure to see, including;

- Horses running to their human when they see them, simply because they want to be together!

- Humans smiling as big or bigger after the session with their horse than they were before!

- Horse/human partnerships working together to move live-stock, teach children, and even save lives through police work, etc.

  Personal Story Update: Now that I have learned what my horse needs and how to provide those needs, my horses meet me at the gate, ready and looking forward to our session together! If I can do it, you can do it!

Understanding the psychology of horses and humans is an important starting point before you begin a journey of changing your horse's behavior. By learning what motivates your horse and what your natural reactions are to his behavior, you will be better able to approach the situations in a way that makes sense to your horse.

How To Get Your Horse In
The "Learning Zone"

To create a willing partner in the horse it is important to understand how and where they learn best. Learning and teaching are such important parts of our lives as horse-men.

In nearly every interaction we have with our horses they are learning something (even if it is something we wished they hadn't learned). Pat says "Everything means 'something,' nothing means 'nothing.'" Once you realize the influence you have in each interaction with your horse you can become a much more aware and effective horse owner.

When we are teaching our horses and spending time with them they most often learn by the release of pressure (whether it is what we intended for them to learn, or not). Very quickly horses will learn what they need to do to get release.

An example of this is; a confident horse who learns if he puts enough pressure on the rope while tied he can get free. The first time it happens it could be by chance, the next time it happens he has started to work out the pattern, and by the third time you can be sure he knows how to get free when tied.

The key to the speed of learning in this example is that the horse is confident and therefore can be in the "Learning Zone." The knowledge of this zone is a powerful tool in understanding your horse and why certain lessons "stick" and why others never seem to.

When horses are in the "Learning Zone" they are incredibly quick to pick up on new patterns and figure out "What happens before what *happens*, happens." Recognizing this zone, noticing when your horse is in it, and not pushing him beyond it, is vitally important to developing a relationship as a trustworthy leader for your horse.

When thinking of your horse's learning zone it may be easier to think in terms that make sense to humans. For example, most people have an area where they feel comfortable such as: at home on the couch. This is an area (mental or physical) where not much learning occurs, we know to a large extent what is going to happen, we feel safe, our needs are met and we are comfortable and content. This is our Comfort Zone.

Just on the outside of our Comfort Zone lives the Learning Zone, this is where things start to feel a little uncomfortable but we can still breath normally and think our way through the situation.

As an example of what it feels like to enter the Learning Zone, interlace your fingers and thumbs together, and notice which thumb is on top. Now, take your fingers apart and bring them back together again, but this time cause the opposite thumb to be on top.

This should feel a little different, maybe weird, but not on the verge of sending you into a panic. This can be what it feels like to step into your Learning Zone: different and a little less comfortable than the Comfort Zone.

Now, let's say someone was with you and they pushed you into doing something you didn't want to or were afraid of doing, something that made you so worried you couldn't think your way out of the situation.

An example of this: A person who is trying to get over the fear of heights and chooses to climb to the top of the Empire State building, but is not yet ready to look over the edge. Their companion proceeds to grab them and hold them at the edge and even a little over the edge. The panic this person would experience and the survival based reaction to do anything to get themselves out of the situation is an example of sending someone to the Panic Zone: a zone about survival and instincts.

Hopefully these examples with human scenarios give you an understanding of the type of zones and feelings I am referring to in the following section.

The following diagram may help to give you a visual of what these zones look like and where they live in relation to each other. It is followed by charts representing the negative and positive effects interactions with our horses can have.

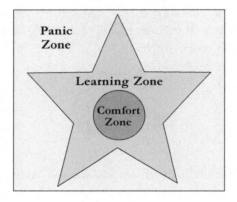

Comfort Zone (circle): This zone represents everywhere your horse is comfortable. This often includes the equine herd, time with their pair bonded buddy horse, the barn, the stall, and hopefully eventually YOU! When referring to this zone as a physical space it is a great place to try new things with your horse. They are already comfortable and relaxed while they are in this zone, so they may be able to stay calmer as a learner while in a physical area that represents comfort.

Learning Zone (star): This area represents the emotional space right outside of your horse's comfort zone. When your horse is in this zone he is still able to think, he is not acting like a terrified prey animal but he is being stretched out of his day-to-day relaxed routine. This is the zone you and your horse need to fall in LOVE with! The more time you can spend with your horse in this zone the deeper and faster your relationship will grow. This zone can also be a physical distance from something, or a mental distance from a task they are already comfortable with.

Panic Zone (square): This is the zone your horse never wants to go to again. This is where they know they are going to lose their life, they become the ultimate prey animal while in this zone. They start to behave in illogical ways – running through fences, running over people, crashing into things and screaming for their herd/barn/pasture. They are in survival mode. Often, time spent in this zone causes your horse to become less confident, and can shrink their comfort zone.

When trying to get horses past the fear of Separation Anxiety there are some common mistakes that are often repeated. Such as trying to force horses to "get over it," or taking the horses away from the herd and working them.

When we make the mistake of pushing our horses and attempting to force them to "get over" emotional issues without the appropriate leadership, we can push them into the PANIC ZONE. At this point and without the necessary skills to help them find comfort again we end up not only making them more resistant to re-enter the LEARNING ZONE but we actually 'shrink' their COMFORT ZONE. This is the opposite of your goal and will not serve you in creating a confident and willing partner who wants to be with you.

Instead, our goal with our horses is to grow their LEARNING ZONE which in effect will also stretch the

COMFORT ZONE. As we help move our horses through exercises with the right psychology behind them, we can cause our horses to become more confident in new environments, more self-confident, and more confident in our leadership.

One of the ways we can help our horses become confident learners is by "Isolating, Separating and Recombining." This is a way of taking the 'problem' and breaking it down into smaller chunks. Little puzzles that our horses can feel successful solving. Each time they successfully solve a puzzle their understanding and communication grows, as well as their confidence in themselves and in us as leaders.

Developing "Confidence Muscles" In Our Horses

While you think of creating a horse that is confident away from his herd and buddy(s) keep in mind that he is a living, breathing being with feelings and the ability to learn and adjust. What this means is that creating a confident horse is not as simple as replacing the oil in a car or changing a tire.

Unlike a car, your horse will have new feelings and make new choices every day. He will learn as he lives and therefore you can think of his confidence more as a muscle than as a set commodity. It is something that can grow OR shrink depending on the attention given to his confidence, the focus of your session, and the 'exercises' you use to develop his confidence.

As you are focused on building your horse's confidence in you as a leader and, therefore, getting him away from his buddy or the herd, remember that this process can be similar to weaning for your horse. His bond with the herd/buddy is a very real and vital connection that is naturally created, one that serves him well when living in 'horse-ville.'

As you build and stretch your horse's comfort away from the herd, keep in mind how strong his innate character influences him to bond with the herd. His calling for his pasture mates is not something he is doing to you in order to embarrass you, or make you have a bad day. When he calls to his herd/buddy he is trying to survive, he is trying to find a way to fulfill his innate needs.

Personal Story: When I first arrived at the Parelli International Study Center in Colorado, my Warmblood mare was leaping in the air, bucking at imaginary flies and pulling me through the arena, while I did a wonderful version of sand skiing! As I looked around at the other 'good' horses, standing still and listening to their humans, I thought "Oh great, I have the WORST horse in the arena! What am I doing here?" It was around this time that over the loud speaker Pat Parelli mentioned what an excellent prey animal my horse was being. He proceeded to say that she was "out thinking, out persisting and out positioning" her human – who was acting like a predator!

We were both doing what we were programmed to do by nature and were not acting like partners. It was an interesting moment because I remember shifting my thinking. All of a sudden I looked at my horse and instead of thinking "What a bad horse!" I thought "You're being an EXCELLENT prey animal!!" From that day on, when my horse began not acting like my partner, I would say to myself "What an excellent prey animal!"

That little phrase changed my approach, and because of the change in approach it changed how my horse saw me. It was the little change in my thinking that helped to make a big change in our relationship. One of my most useful tools to this day is the thought "You're being an excellent prey animal."

If your horse is very strongly bonded to the herd, you can

make progress and he can learn self-confidence away from the herd, but remember you are developing a new skill.

Your horse is an excellent prey animal and you both have to learn how to think like partners. This new skill is much like a new "muscle." You can make this self-confidence muscle strong and healthy, but it can quickly shrink (meaning that once you have developed a horse with a big "Comfort Zone," he may not keep that comfort zone for life).

Sometimes all it takes is a trailer ride with another horse, or an overnight in a stall next to another horse, for your horse to revert back to acting like an excellent prey animal. If this happens and you have prepared and practiced your patterns at home, when you arrive at the clinic/show/trail and your horse is acting like he's never been apart from his buddy; take a deep breath and get ready to build positive patterns, AGAIN.

The good news is that the more often and more successfully you build positive patterns away from the other horses – in every situation – the less time it will take the next time.

Another important piece of the puzzle is the timing of your release. Horses are brilliant at figuring out what happens, before what *happens*, happens. This means they are great at learning patterns and they quickly figure out how to find release.

As the leader what this means to you is that you need to be aware of WHEN you are releasing pressure. If you release when things are not going well because you are frustrated, then you have just 're-enforced' the behavior your horse offered, which reinforces the undesirable behavior.

In each session with your horse it is powerful to keep in mind your overall goal for the day: such as 'confidence,' 'lightness of response,' or 'desire to be with you.' The important part is that whatever you pick you reward your horse for moving towards that goal. During your session this will usually look like many 'mini-releases' and then ending the session on a great effort.

A mini-release might be something as small as taking away the pressure or stimulus for a breath, or saying "good boy," or whatever fits you and your horse. The concept of mini-releases can be very useful when you are asking your horse to do something for an extended period of time, for example: backing a circle around the entire barn. In this circumstance you will need to give mini-releases along the way so that your horse knows he is on the right track and continues to put in effort. The BIG release will usually come once he has put in a lot of extra effort, or when you've completed the task.

Keeping the release in mind can help you know when to end your session. There will be days when everything goes completely wrong and it seems nothing could go right. On these days, find something you and your horse are good at, even if it is just walking back to the herd and petting him, and end on that.

Remember that your overall goal is to build a relationship with your horse that motivates him to be with you. He would rather be with someone who takes him to the herd and rubs him, than someone who leaves angry or upset.

The following article I wrote was originally published in the Parelli *Savvy Times* magazine and may offer some insight into how great it can be when you have a horse that is "herd-bound!" Regardless of what some people may say, there are wonderful things about herd-bound horses, specifically their strength of desire to BOND.

Separation Anxiety Or A High Propensity For Bonding?

As I mentioned in the previous section; the first year I studied at the Parelli Center in Pagosa Springs, Colorado, Pat Parelli said something that changed my Horsemanship. "Your horse is being an excellent prey animal." This is one of those sayings that has stuck with me and I think of it often as I play with all Horsenalities.

However, when I first heard it I smiled and thought "yah, thanks!" (note the sarcasm!), but over the next few months what it helped me realize is that the more frustrated I was with my horse the better prey animal she was. This meant that even though I felt like everything was going WRONG, in actual fact my horse was doing the one job she was programmed to do, perfectly!!

She was acting like an EXCELLENT prey animal! What I mean by this is that in order for horses to survive they have to out-think, out-maneuver and out-persist us predators, and boy was my horse good at out-thinking the predator on the end of her rope.

Each time I remember this saying it brings a smile to my face because the less a horse is doing FOR the predator (human) the better prey animal they are being. Now, the true addiction and art of horsemanship comes when we both – horse and human – stop acting the way we are programmed to and start acting like partners. This partnership is what draws us to horses; it can be so rewarding that as horsemen we will do almost anything to keep our ultimate partner, the horse, in our lives.

Recently this quote resurfaced during a Parelli tour event. Pat was just getting started with the demonstration horse, a very athletic and attractive mare. The owner had just walked out of the arena and Pat took the halter off and let the horse loose. The horse was looking outside the arena for safety and comfort. Pat began playing the *Catching Game* and explaining to the audience what he was doing.

As he played, the horse was putting all of its energy into searching outside the arena. In the next moment Pat made a comment about this horse having an excellent ability to bond. Which stumped many in the audience – they were watching this horse look everywhere but to Pat, and he was complimenting the horse on its propensity to bond!

Pat shone a light on how hard the horse was looking away and helped the audience realize that in this moment the horse wasn't being 'bad,' she was acting like an excellent prey animal. In fact, the amount of effort she was putting into looking away from him showed how much she wanted to bond with something/someone. She just didn't realize that it could be with Pat – yet.

In a matter of minutes she was following Pat around the arena and even trotting after him! All that energy she had put into doing the opposite of what he asked actually showed what a great partner she could be.

This transition in thinking that Pat showed is such a key element to horsemanship. The first step to getting the changes in our horse we desire is often a change in our thinking!

This example can even show up when we take our horses to new environments, clinics, shows, camps, etc. Often horses are screaming to find the herd, whinnying in a new environment, running around us in circles, while we are trying to focus on why we are at the event. This is a very frustrating 'problem' because we are trying to learn and they (our horse) are acting like a freak! It's embarrassing because attention is being drawn towards us at the end of the rope, and frustrating because we can't think with all the screaming – AND no one around us can learn either.

What if in this moment you could think "You are acting like an EXCELLENT prey animal!" If you (as the leader) change the way you think you will change the way you act. If in this moment you become someone worth following your horse will become your partner. Just like the demo horse did with Pat.

Knowing this and knowing that each horse is being excellent at what they are programmed to do, our next task becomes creating patterns in our horses that will serve them in "Humansville," where they live today. The patterns we instill need to build confidence in horses AWAY from their herd (Self Confidence), which is very unnatural for a programmed herd animal.

These patterns also need to build trust and communication with humans (the ultimate predator); again, very unnatural for the ultimate prey animal. In short, the patterns you build with your horse need to help him become smarter, braver, calmer, and more athletic, as well as create a willingness to use these talents in partnership with you, vs. outthinking you! Pat did this by showing up as a leader for the horse in the arena. He matched the horse's energy and each time the horse looked for safety on the outside of the arena, Pat helped her focus back towards him. In the moment this built her confidence in him as a leader.

Another approach is to build patterns before the event, clinic/show/camp/etc. that create confidence in your horse away from the herd, to increase your horse's Self Confidence. Helping them increase their bubble of comfort and confidence to eat, sleep, and rest while away from their pasture mates. Also, after establishing patterns you can add variety by changing the location of the pattern, thus increasing confidence in new environments.

If we can approach situations where things aren't going as we planned as learning opportunities, and ways for us to step up as the leader our horses need, we can see life from their perspective. This is an opportunity for us to turn frustrations into fascinations. Our horses are not acting like freaks and idiots to create stress in our lives; they are acting like an excellent prey animal.

Our goal as a leader is much like the goal of parents or teachers: to help expand the student's bubble. To stretch our students out of their comfort zones enough to cause growth.

Without stretching, growth will not occur – if we always do what we've always done, we'll always get what we've always gotten. This means that for us and our horses there will be moments where things are uncomfortable, but this can mean progress.

The mastery of horsemanship comes from finding the balance between pushing our horses over the 'edge,' and staying comfortable in the same place we've always been.

Our aim is to find the place that is just right; where reaching for progress expands our horse's ability mentally, emotionally, and physically – without pushing too far and causing fear and anxiety.

The question to ponder is: are you striving to become the leader your horse needs; a person who not only loves them, but helps to teach them the skills needed to become an ultimate partner in Humansville, and not just an excellent prey animal? Because, in the end, there's nothing you can't do when your horse becomes a part of you!

Creating New Patterns

...eate a new pattern with your horse you need to be ready to build a PROGRAM. By building a program you will help solidify the new behavior for your horse. At the same time you will be building his 'self-confidence muscle,' as well as his incentive and motivation to leave the herd/barn.

This program starts by practicing the new pattern seven days in a row (this also could be classified as seven sessions in a row, as long as the sessions are not spaced too far apart). Then, practicing the same thing every other day for a week (every other play session for the next seven sessions). Then every once in a while.

Keep in mind that with herd-bound horses they are practicing the pattern of having all their needs met by the herd/stall for up to 24 hours a day when you are not with them. This is a lot of time that your horse gets to practice the pattern you are trying to change!

By taking the time to build a program you are building a strong new pattern to reshape previous behaviors. Be patient, and if you fall off of your program, just start again. Remember you are going through this process to build a better and stronger relationship with your horse, not to race to the finish line. It will not save you time or energy to shortcut the process now. *Take the time it takes.*

The very last section of this book contains some sheets to help you keep track of your progress while building these new pattern programs. You will be able to check off each time you complete a session as well as keep track of how long it took you to complete seven sessions.

For example, it will be more meaningful for your horse if you did seven sessions, seven days in a row, versus taking one month to complete seven sessions.

Creating An Icon Of Safety

As you play with your horse and create new patterns of relaxation and comfort away from the herd, you can also think of creating an 'Icon of Safety' for your horse. You can do this by making of pattern of safety, comfort, and food at an object, on a pattern, or with you.

For example, if you chose to use the Parelli Figure 8 pattern as your icon of safety, your horse would begin finding comfort and relaxation as soon as they were on the pattern. You would use this pattern in your program and reward your horse when they found relaxation on the pattern. This pattern could then work for you as a 'Safety Blanket' when you go into new environments. If your horse were to get worried, you could start them on the familiar figure 8 pattern and it can help them find relaxation.

You can create this same icon of safety with a pedestal, cones, barrels, anything you choose – even yourself. This is one of the reasons why horses are so bonded with their mothers and the herd. The other horses provide safety, comfort, play, and access to food. As you play and focus on creating an icon of safety, think of creating a bond so strong that it resembles the reassurance found between a mare and foal.

This is what great leaders do for their horses, they create safety, comfort, play, and food with themselves, as the leader. For the horse, this translates to the human being the leader AND an icon of safety. This means that when the horse becomes worried, they can look to the human for safety, similar to a foal looking to its mother.

By using the exercises in this book, you will begin to develop your horse's association with YOU as the leader and icon of safety. This will make moving into new environments easier and smoother for both you and your horse. Your horse will not have as much anxiety in new environments because YOU will know his needs and be capable of providing those needs.

A Note On Tying

Another way to help your horse develop patience and to find comfort away from the herd can be to set up a pattern of tying. This is a strategy that, when used with savvy, can help a horse learn how to be calm on his own, without you or the herd. This is particularly useful in situations where there is a horse left behind who 'worries' about his herd mates when they are gone. If used correctly it will develop confidence in your horse while helping him become accustomed to – and confident in – spending time away from the herd.

As with any of the approaches you take with your horse it is important to remember to gradually stretch his comfort zone. Keep in mind that new patterns are most useful when presented in a way that keeps your horse in the learning zone.

As leaders it is up to us to see things from our horse's perspective FIRST, as opposed to looking only from our limited personal perspective. Even though, as humans, we can look at the situation and 'see' nothing is going to hurt our horses and everything will be fine, it is vital to building a quality relationship that we recognize the horse's perspective, and that they may view the situation entirely differently. By taking notice of this you can offer your horse a progressive approach to tying that builds his comfort zone, rather than shrinking it.

It is entirely up to you whether or not you choose to incorporate a program of tying into your program. However, if you choose to use tying as a pattern, keep in mind some general safety tips:

- Be sure your horse can yield to steady pressure, even in an "Oh No!" situation. This means that even when your horse is fearful he knows how to come off pressure and will not hurt himself by pulling back.

- Be sure you are tying to something safe and strong (you do not want your horse to be able to pull the thing you tie to out and have it drug behind him).

- Remember to tie your horse high. When you tie your horse from something higher than his withers he will not be able to get as much leverage as he would when tied to something lower (this means your horse will stay safer).

- Keep the rope short. The rope needs to be short enough that your horse can't get a leg over it, and long enough that he can rest his head comfortably. In general it is unsafe to tie your horse long enough to eat grass.

Keeping these things in mind will help you create a safe environment to tie your horse.

Also, be sure that your horse is in a safe Zone to be tied. It is not appropriate to tie a horse that is in his Panic Zone; horses are prey animals and can easily get hurt in this situation.

You want to set your horse up for success, so be sure you have built some patterns away from the herd where your horse knows how to find comfort and relaxation. Ideally when you first start a tying program, your horse's herd will still be within eyesight. You will practice building his confidence bubble away from the herd just as you have done with the other exercises.

Using Multiple Exercises In A Session

While you are focusing on creating a pattern, you do not have to get stuck doing just one exercise per session. The overall goal is creating a situation where your horse finds comfort with you and away from his herd/stall/buddy.

Some days you may play with one to five, or more, exercises in the same session to get your horse focused on you. More exercises will help keep your left-brained (or easily bored) horse engaged in the session. Right-brained (more fearful and skeptical) horses will gain confidence in the consistency of repeating the same exercise to create a pattern.

The key to creating a pattern of bonding is when you quit. "It's not so much what you do, as when you stop doing it that counts." This quote from Pat Parelli is valuable to keep in mind as you play. The best time to quit during your session is when you have built a stronger connection and more trust with your horse (more than you had at the start of the day/session). If you keep your goal in mind, it will help you know when to quit the session (you might even have more than one session a day to fast track your progress).

Of course there will be times when you aren't able to quit at the best possible moment (time constraints, outside emergency, pushing a little too far, etc.), but the important thing to remember is, if you are able, end in a place where you can both feel SUCCESSFUL.

Aim at ending in a successful place even if you have to go back to the herd/stall/buddy and simply play the Friendly Game. The important thing is that your horse begins to see you as someone who provides him with what he needs AND wants.

As you become familiar with the theory, the exercises, and the approach, you can incorporate the information into your normal sessions with your horse. The timing of your release will become more refined and you will be able to reward for the relationship and bond, as well as rewarding for the behavior.

The Catching Game And Creating Draw

As you think about developing a great relationship with your horse, one of the things that makes a big shift in the relationship is the words we use when talking about our horses. For example, replacing the words "make" and "let" with "CAUSE" and "ALLOW;" and "breaking colts" with "STARTING HORSES."

Another area we can create a huge impact is when we think of catching our horses. What if we could get our horses to catch us? Rather than going out to the field to catch your horse, could you go out and have your horse catch you? In any of the catching games you play with horses this is a fundamental concept: creating draw so that your horse will want to be with you.

There are many ways you can approach this puzzle. First, Pat Parelli has created a Catching Game, which is most useful when taught in a round pen. The basic guidelines to remember when playing are: if you have no eyes from the horse, create pressure; if you have one eye from the horse, create a little pressure; if you have two eyes from the horse, take off pressure.

Second, you can think of how you want to create more draw. The solution to this puzzle is thinking about what your horse likes and needs, then providing those things in a way that your horse recognizes you as the 'bringer of good things.'

Some examples of things your horse may like are: grass, grain, scratches, rest, treats, water, etc. Almost everyg your horse needs fits into the categories of SAFETY, MFORT, PLAY, or FOOD.

Being able to provide horses with what they need, when they need it, can deepen your bond and relationship. It allows you to give them the things they need in exchange for the wonderful things they 'give' you in return, sometimes even just that delightful horsey smell!

You can think of the things that motivate your horse as being a teeter totter, each location or environment he finds Safety, Comfort, Play and Food in, increases his draw to that situation again.

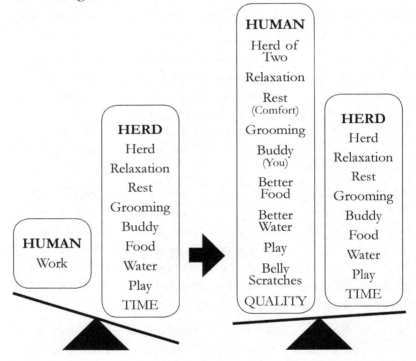

Often the only thing horses get with people is work or stress, this leaves the human side of the teeter totter very "light" in the horse's mind, there often isn't much desire to be with the human again.

On the flip side when our horses are turned out to pasture or in a herd environment they are able to find; Safety, Comfort, Play, and Food. This makes the "herd" side of the teeter totter very "heavy"!

Another thing that influences the teeter totter in your relationship is the number of hours your horse spends getting his needs met by the herd. This is a HUGE factor in how much draw he has towards the herd. Unless you live with your horse, this means that the QUALITY of things you provide for your horse will have to be higher, so that you can influence the teeter totter in your direction.

As you incorporate this concept into your sessions your goal can be to first balance the teeter totter and with diligence you will even be able to cause the human side to become heavier!

As you play your way through the exercises in this book, also see if you can implement some of your horse's motivators (the things he likes) into your sessions. If he can begin to see that you provide things he enjoys you are likely to begin the positive pattern of causing your horse to catch you.

Building your HERD OF TWO

One of the great motivators for a horse is being in a herd as it is where he feels the safest and most at ease. An excellent way to develop a horse that is confident with you is to help him see you as his herd. When he associates you as his herd, you will be able to provide what he needs through the Seven Games.

In fact, everything we do with our horses (when we are communicating naturally) is centered around the Seven Games. Pat Parelli says everything we do with our horses is one of or a combination of the Seven Games. In addi-

of the Seven Games, there are really only 3 (Friendly, cupine, & Driving). After understanding the Seven Games a variation in what we ask and get from our horses comes down to when and what we are rewarding. In the following exercises our goal is to reward our horse's connection to us and his confidence away from the equine herd/barn. This can only happen when he begins to see us (the human) as part of his herd.

Horses are seeking a herd. They are created to find a herd to keep them safe, this can range from a herd of 2 to 25+. The important part is that the herd has a leader and at least one follower. What this means is that you can create a herd of two. Together, horse and human, make up a herd of two, us (the human) functioning as the leader and the horse as the follower.

The exercises following the theory section are designed to give you creative ways to use the Seven Games to develop a stronger relationship with your horse, as well as helping you plan the location of your horse's relaxation. By doing this you will help your horse become more confident with you as his leader at the same time you develop his confidence away from his herd.

Ending A Session

At the completion of each repetition through an exercise you are asked to take your horse to the appropriate distance (the distance your horse is ready for) away from the herd. You will be gradually increasing this distance from 6 feet to 150 yards or more. This is one of the times you can add in some extra incentive for your horse. You could add special feeds, special water, scratches, treats, etc. Adding a program of providing feed and water can help to deepen the bond with your horse. If you are the provider of the things your horse needs and wants, your horse's relationship with you starts to hold more value. In some extreme cases you can even be the sole provider of certain things such as water (if you choose to do this, be sure you are taking your horse to water often enough to keep him healthy and if you have any concerns, consult your veterinarian). The pattern of your horse seeing you and then being taken to something he needs can be a strong reinforcer to the value of your relationship.

Another important detail to remember as your horse's partner and leader is where you finish your session for the day. After spending time creating a situation where you are the "bringer of good things," the last thing you want to do is leave your horse in an area he is uncomfortable. For example if you will be turning your horse back out to the pasture, take him to the herd before letting him go. This way his last thought of you is relaxation and being somewhere comfortable when you leave. However, if you short cut the process and turn him loose at the gate, leaving him to run back to his herd, his last thought of you will be mixed with the discomfort of being left alone, having to get his adrenaline up to find his herd and then finding safety and comfort again with the herd (the exact pattern we are trying to change).

Me And My Shadow Game: Prerequisite To Getting Started

Originally developed by Linda Parelli and taught as part of a 6 week long course at the Parelli Centers, "Me and My Shadow" can be a valuable game. If you are willing to open your mind and see what your horse shows you, this game can help you get a deeper understanding of what your horse is motivated by, his innate Horsenality, and build his acceptance of you as his partner. I suggest you use this game as a pre-requisite to the exercises outlined in this book, it will give insight into your horse, and is a great way to start a fresh and more meaningful relationship with him.

The basic principles of "Me and My Shadow" are:

Zone 3: You will be sticking with your horse by putting your arm over his back (Zone 3). If he is too tall for you to reach, you can play the game by putting your stick over his back. The benefit of having your arm over his back include;

• Feeling how his breathing changes in new environments

• You will be able to feel if he is tight or tense

• You can learn what happens in his body before what happens, happens. Meaning, what does he do before he gets impulsive? What does he do before he stops? Etc.

49/51% Leadership

A partnership where you transfer leadership back and forth; at times you will hold 51% of the leadership (with the horse having 49%), at times your horse will hold 51% of the leadership (with you having 49%). What this means is that you are going to be allowing your horse to make choices while you follow, and learn what he chooses. At the same time you will be setting guidelines for him to make choices within. These are guidelines that you feel able to follow. For example you may choose to follow him as long as he stays at walk or as long as he stays calm and thinking.

Safety

Ultimately you are the leader in this situation, so if your horse is getting into an unsafe situation, it is your responsibility to take back 51% leadership and help bring him back to a safer situation.

Speed

You get to pick the top speed for this exercise. What this means is that if you want a great workout you can choose to allow your horse to travel at any speed up to a trot! However, I suggest a maximum speed of: walk. Sticking with your horse at walk allows you to become more aware of your surroundings and his reaction to them. In this exercise you are only able to dictate your horse's top speed, what this means is that you are to go as SLOW as your horse wants to go! This is how you will learn about the edges of your horse's comfort zone. Horses, when given a choice will often stay in their comfort zone and occasionally take trips to the learning zone (if they get bored in the comfort zone). Also, when given the freedom to choose horses will often explore their surroundings, once they feel safe. Sometimes they may even self-regulate their approach to new objects and area. They begin to create their own game of approach and retreat, to build their own confidence.

If your horse comes to a complete stop, and has been

stopped for at least 7 seconds, you can go through your Phases and ask him to move forward again. These Phases will look like;

1. Bring your life and energy up and look forward

2. Lift your arm over your horse's back

3. Bring your arm down and begin tapping with rhythm

4. Continue upping the intensity of the rhythm until he takes a step forward

5. GO TO NEUTRAL and follow him

Step 5 is the most important, you want to go to neutral as soon as he takes a step, if he only makes it one step before stopping again, WAIT at least 7 seconds, then ask for one more step and repeat.

If you have an introverted horse this is going to be a slow game. If you have an extroverted horse you will get good at disengaging the HQ (yielding them away until you get two eyes looking at you) and starting over when he runs past you (by doing this as a pattern it will help your horse learn that running past you is uncomfortable and more work than staying beside you). It also allows your horse the freedom to move his feet quickly if he needs to, so that you do not have to block him. The disengage is where you will get control back and allows you to reposition yourself.

What To Look For

As you play there are so many things you can be observant towards and therefore learn about your horse, for example:

*What kind of grass is his favorite? (This will serve you well when you a choosing a place to reward in the next section, after an exercise).

* What are the things he chooses to avoid? (This will give you feedback into the edges of his comfort zone)

* Is he drawn to anything? (This will help you learn what he is motivated by)

* How quickly does he move forward, given a choice? (This may shine a light on his Horsenality)

* Is his head high or low? (This can give insight into his Horsenality).

* Does he seem confident to explore or more worried in the environment? (This can give insight into tendency towards right brain and left brain behavior)

Of course there are many more things you will learn, but hopefully the above has given you a few things to think about as well as sparking your imagination.

Personal Story: I have a Thoroughbred/Quarter Horse mare. The first time I played Me and My Shadow I started in her pen (stall) with the gate open. I realized she was a Right Brained Introvert and so I figured it would take some time before she wanted to leave her pen. I was guessing a day or two before she will feel self-confident enough to leave the pen with me just following along. I was very curious to see how long it would take and decided to diligently play the game as instructed and allow her to choose where and how fast we would play. I played every day for 6 weeks. During the 5th week she finally left her stall. WOW!!! Did I learn a lot about her! She was even more unconfident in new areas then I thought and she was a very unconfident learner! I had been doing things with her in the past and because she was obedient she had been doing what I wanted, but when I left the decision up to her it took a LONG time for her to choose to take a step out of her comfort zone. HOW INTERESTING! This changed how a played with her, I slowed things WAY down, took more time when introducing something new and noticed the little signs she was giving me (tight lips, shallow breathing, etc.) that she wasn't ready to go farther. The result was a horse that by the end of the 6th week was whinnying to me when she saw me approach her pen. She was meeting me at the gate for her halter and ready to come out right away. That one game gave me more understanding for her than 10 books could have. She was such a great teacher for me!

Although you may have an extroverted horse, this game can still offer a lot to your relationship. It can build your horse's trust in you, it can help him accept you as a passenger and partner, and it's a great way to give your horse a chance to express himself before starting to ask him to perform for you. Me and My Shadow is a great tool to help you understand your horse's perspective first.

Horse's Body Language

As you progress through the exercises in the next section it is important that you understand how to "read your horse." Particularly, how to tell if he is thinking about the herd or would rather be somewhere else (instead of with you).

The following chart gives some clues on things to observe in your horse, so you can tell if he is making positive changes towards seeing you as his herd of two. Keep in mind you want to reward signs of relaxation and bonding with you.

The behaviors in the following column are some general tips on how to tell if your horse is relaxed and confident.

	UNconfident	Confident
EYES	Wide	Soft
	Not Blinking	Blinking
EARS	Stiff/Rigid	Soft & "bendable"
	Darting	Slowly moving
MOUTH	Tight	Soft and floppy
	Wrinkled	Licking and Chewing
NECK	High	Close to or
	Rigid	lower than withers
BODY/ MUSCLES	Stiff & locked	Soft
BREATHING	Shallow	Deep, steady
	Irregular or Fast	
FEET	Moving	Still and relaxed
	Ready to move	Leg cocked
TAIL	"J" shape	Easy to move around
	High tail	Hanging/swinging freely
	Tight	
	(hard to move)	

How To Get Started

1. Remember as you get ready for any event, preparation is key. The most important thing to your horse is that you understand the theory and adjust your sessions with your horse to build his confidence away from the herd, trust and respect for your leadership and the timing of your release. Complete at least one session of "Me and My Shadow" to start.

2. Choose the section that most closely resembles how your horse is kept: Pasture, Stall, Buddy, and play your way through the section.

3. Keep track of your sessions using the Partner Progress Pages to chart your program and consistency in building a pattern with your horse.

4. After completing the exercises in your section you may find it useful to use additional sections and adjust the exercises to fit your situation. These sections can give you additional tools and perspectives for continuing to build your relationship. Please include the exercises in the Riding section, keeping track of your program on the Partner Progress Pages.

5. Read over the Emergency Strategy section so you will be better prepared for unforeseen situations when they arise.

6. Keep in mind the theory, and rewarding your horse for the behavior you want are the most useful pieces to add to your training. The exercises simply give you a framework to use to get the results you want with your horse.

GET STARTED, have FUN and ENJOY THE JOURNEY!!

SECTION 1

Horses Kept In The Pasture In A Herd

Strategies for building Confidence in your horse
when separating them from the herd.
These techniques will be most relevant for horses
that are kept in a pasture setting.
In addition you can use most of the exercises
from horses "Kept In Pairs."

...orsenality Filter: Horses Kept In A Herd

...ı progress through the following section you may find ...orsenality filter below useful to help tailor each exercise ...your individual horse.

LB Extrovert

- PLAY!
- Be effective with Phases.
- Drive Zone 1.
- Choose exercises where your horse is moving his feet on a long line away from you, such as Exercises 7, 9, 10, 12, 13, 14, 15 and 16.
- You may need to rotate between several exercises.

RB Extrovert

- This horse is looking for SAFETY.
- They need patterns and consistency to learn.
- Keep moving their feet until they are CALM.
- Choose exercises that move their feet on a long line without creating too much adrenaline (for now), such as Exercises 2, 3, 4, 5, 6, 7, 9, 11 and 15.

LB Introvert

- MOTIVATION is very important for this horse.
- Be quick with your release, and give them responsibilities.
- This horse thinks best when his feet are still.
- Choose exercises that start by moving one foot at a time, go slow to build interest, such as Exercises 1, 2, 4, 6, 8, 10, 11, 13, and 14.

RB Introvert

- This horse is seeking COMFORT.
- Be ready to WAIT for a lick and chew after they learn something new or relax.
- This horse thinks best when they aren't moving.
- Choose exercises that include a small amount of motion then rest to build trust and relaxation, such as Exercises 1, 2, 5, 6, 8, 11, and 13.

Safety Reminders

Be aware of other horses in the herd, keep yourself safe, and be sure you don't ask your horse to go too close to a dominant horse. Be careful introducing food as incentive in this environment, it may bring out the herd dominance. Also, be sure you are safe in the herd environment, and aware of not only yourself and your horse but also the additional horses in the herd, before you try any of these exercises. If you aren't ready to keep track of all these factors, you may need to modify so that the fence is between you and the herd.

Catching Game Tips For The Herd Environment

Remember the concept of two eyes – no pressure, one eye – a little pressure, no eyes – pressure. At the same time be aware of your effect on the herd. You may need to go up to the easiest horse to catch first and work your way around to the horse you want. Stay safe and ask for help before you put yourself in an unsafe situation. You may need to take time establishing a good catching game, away from the following exercises, before trying the catching game with your horse in the herd.

Ways To Reward Your Horse Away From The Herd

Rest, scratches, food, water/molasses water. Be very aware of the effect of treats/food/water on the herd. It may be best to skip this type of reward if it will create an unsafe situation for you or your horse in their herd environment.

Suggestions For Steps To Build Your Distance Away From The Herd Within Each Exercise

Start at 12', next time 15', 22', 32', 45', other side of paddock, rest outside paddock, rest in the barn, rest in the arena, rest in the trailer, rest on the other side of the barn, etc.

Recommendations For Your Level Of Savvy

Adjust the exercise to fit your savvy level (including rope lengths, distance away from your horse, and the skills/sequence of the exercise). For example: Level 1 – 12' line, Level 2 – 22' line, Levels 3 and 4 – 45' line. Each exercise has a list of pre-requisites. If you do not yet have the level of savvy suggested for that exercise you may choose to wait until later.

Helpful References

Parelli Zones Of The Horse for reference as you read through the following section.

Seven Games Summary And Reminders

Principle Games

1. **Friendly Game:** This game is the Confidence Game – to help your horse gain confidence in people, places, changes and things. While playing this game you will use:

   • *Approach and Retreat* • *Rhythm.*

2. **Porcupine Game:** This game is focused around the concept of teaching your horse to *Follow a Feel.*

3. **Driving Game:** This game is about getting your horse to *Follow a Suggestion.*

Purpose Games

4. **Yo-Yo Game:** The to and fro game. By using this game you help your horse balance *Backwards and Forwards.*

5. **Circling Game:** The purpose of circling to help your horse learn his *Responsibilities.*

6. **Sideways Game:** This game is all about *Lateral Movements.*

7. **Squeeze Game:** Also known as the *Matador Game.* This game is about *Shortening Your Horse's Flight Line* and helping them build confidence in situations they perceive as a Squeeze or as claustrophobic.

1. Yielding To And Fro

Prerequisites
- Tying the halter knot.
- Catching your horse.
- Safety in the herd environment.

Outcomes (When to quit)
- Lightness on the halter; 6-8 ounces of pressure to respond.
- More attention on you than the other horses.
- Practicing Friendly Game to Porcupine Game and back again.

Steps
1. Get your horse to catch you, then put the halter on. (Refer to "catching game" in the theory section for more information). You can keep your horse where he is in the herd (as long as you are safe) while you play this game.

2. Use Porcupine Game off of the halter to back horse five steps. Rub after he backs.

3. Use Porcupine off of the halter to bring horse forwards five steps. Rub.
4. Repeat three to five times and then take horse away from herd to rest.

Savvy Tips

- Other variations/additions of this exercise include: lowering head off of Porcupine pressure/raise up from pressure under the jaw, Sideways away by Porcupining Zone 3, ropes around Zone 3 to yield towards, lead by the ear.
- Remember your Porcupine Phases (hair, skin, muscle, bone), rub (Friendly Game) – stimulate (Porcupine Game) – rub (Friendly Game).

Troubleshooting

- *My horse bites me when I try to back him up.*
  Try one of the exercises that uses Driving Game where your horse is farther away from you; also review the Horsenality information – you may need to Drive Zone 1 more before your horse is ready for Porcupine.
- *My horse doesn't want to rest when away from the herd, he keeps moving his feet.*
  Great! This means he's ready to do more, go ahead and move on to some of the exercises later in this section and/ or the exercises recommended for extroverts.
- *My horse won't move!*
  After going through your Phases, keep the pressure of Phase 4 Porcupine while you add Driving Game to support. As soon as he moves, release.

Ways To Advance This Exercise

- See if you can get your horse to yield backwards and forwards with your hand on his nose. Ask him to yield backwards off the pressure, keep your hand in position as a Friendly Game, and see if he will walk forward towards your hand. This is a great game to play and can help build to riding with contact.

51

2. Zone 3 "Touch It"

Prerequisites
- Safety in the herd environment.
- Understanding Phases of Driving Game and Friendly Game.
- A basic understanding of the game "Touch It."

Outcomes
- Horse focused more on you than the herd; looking towards you and responding to your requests.
- Be able to direct your horse effectively from Zone 3 and stay in Zone 3 while going from point to point.
- Equal response from both sides.

Steps

1. With your halter and 12-foot line on your horse, stand in Zone 3 and begin Driving your horse to a target just on the outside of the herd.

2. Once you get there, stop and rest for 30-90 seconds. If your horse wants to eat – that's great!
3. Pick a new object that takes you right past the herd and allows you to rest on the other side of the herd. Allow

your horse to rest while facing away from the herd.

4. Repeat the exercise to the same object two times, then pick a new spot a little further away, and repeat. Keep playing until your horse is focused on you, then allow your horse a big reward away from the herd.

Savvy Tips

• Be aware of your horse's learning zone in relation to the herd and do not ask him to go too far away from the herd too soon.

• For more information on Driving from Zone 3 and Touch It games, check the Parelli Program.

• Pick objects that will be comfortable for your horse to stop at and rest.

Troubleshooting

• *My horse is scared of the object I chose.*

For this exercise pick a new object, or switch your focus to Friendly Game. In this exercise we are trying to build your horse's comfort zone away from the herd, not necessarily addressing Friendly Game with obstacles.

• *My horse walked past the object I chose.*

That's okay, disengage the HQ and send him back towards it (Pat Parelli's never seen this take longer than two days!), also be sure you are using your body language to direct him to the object.

• *My horse will not walk forward.*

Go through your Phases of Driving Game (direct him with your energy and focus, pick your stick up off his back, add rhythmic pressure with your stick, increase the intensity and release when he takes a step).

Ways To Advance This Exercise

• Begin increasing the distance you are away from your horse so you can still communicate. Build the distance from 2 feet to 40+ feet. This will test your communication and respect.

3. Backwards Around The Herd's Bubble

Prerequisites
- Knowledge of your safety in the herd, as a first priority. Only do this exercise if you are safe in the pasture with the herd.
- Level 1 Driving Game skills with your Carrot Stick.

Outcomes
- Horse focused more on you than the herd; shown by calling less to the herd.
- Backwards with lightness and responsiveness, Phase 2 or 3.
- Ability to steer your horse while going backwards.

Steps

1. Use Driving Game (rhythmic pressure) to back your horse.

2. As you back your horse, drive him so that he is backing in a large circle around the herd (following the shape of the herd's "bubble").

54

3. Continue backing, giving small releases when he puts in the slightest try.

4. When he is focused on you, back him away from the herd and give him a BIG release.

Savvy Tips
- Keep a strong focus on where you are going.
- Give your horse a short rest when he puts in effort to backing.
- Use your Driving Game on the HQ to direct the tail in a circle, thinking of steering like you would with a wheelbarrow.

Troubleshooting
- *My horse won't back!*
  Go through your Phases and be sure to release on the slightest try.
- *My horse keeps backing crooked.*
  He's not thinking backwards yet. Keep asking and be just with your Phases. Expect a lot, accept a little, and reward often — if he puts effort into going "straighter" for even ONE step, give him a rest.

"The better your horse is at backwards and sideways, the better he will be at everything else."–Pat Parelli

4. "Stop Sign:" Backwards

Prerequisites
• Safety in the herd environment.
• Level 1-2 forequarter (FQ) yields.
• 'Stick To Me' backwards from Zone 2.   .

Outcomes
• Horse focused more on you than the herd; less calling to the herd.
• Achieving backwards while you stay in Zone 3.
• Your horse respectfully yielding the FQ.

Steps

1. Play Friendly Game and move into your horse's Zone 2.

2. From Zone 2 ask your horse to back up next to you ('Stick To Me' style).
3. Once he is smoothly backing, turn towards him, drive the front end over two steps, then resume your parallel position to your horse (as in step 2) and back him 5-7 steps.

4. Repeat this exercise, making an octagon around the herd. When you feel his attention is on you, back him away from the herd and allow him to rest.

Savvy Tips

- FOCUS! Your focus is key here. When asking your horse to back, focus in the distance (your shoulders mirroring your horse's). When you drive the front end over – turn your shoulders to face your horse and look over his neck where you want him to go.
- The goal is to get your horse responding to your energy and focus, don't use the stick if you don't have to.

Troubleshooting

- *My horse won't yield his FQ away.*
  Use your Driving Game Phases. Also, have a clear idea of what you want, and reward him as soon as he gets closer to what you are asking.

Ways To Advance This Exercise

- Keep in mind your goal is to have your horse responding off just your intention. See if your horse can follow your focus, move backwards, and yield his FQ without you ever needing to lift the Carrot Stick.

5. Yielding The HQ Until You Get The Other Eye

Prerequisites
- Safety in the herd environment.
- Level 1 Driving Game FQ and HQ skills.

Outcomes
- Horse focused more on you than the herd; little to no calling to the other horses.
- You and your horse flowing from HQ to FQ yielding without loss of rhythm.

Steps

1. Play Friendly Game and position yourself beside Zone 3.

2. Drive the hindquarter (HQ) until your horse is yielding away smoothly.

3. Allow room (with your shoulder that is closest to the horse) and drive the HQ far enough that your horse's nose passes in front of you.

4. Do this several times in a flow. Now, once your horse switches eyes, drive the FQ for a step or two. When your horse is focused on you, drive him away from the herd and rest.

Savvy Tips
• Keep Driving the HQ until your horse offers to bring his nose across in front of you – the key is that he offers, not that you make it happen.
• Be sure you are making a space between your horse's shoulder and your shoulder so that he has room to bring his nose through the "open door."

Troubleshooting
• *My horse won't bring his nose past me.*
  Be sure you are giving him enough space, also remember to go through your Phases of Driving Game and be effective. Last, stick with it – it may take a full circle or three before he tries something new.
• *I feel like I am too close to my horse.*
  As you are Driving the HQ, think of making an arc out and around to get from his nose to his HQ (like a rainbow), this will help him to see you and keep you at a safe distance.

6. Yo-Yo Game

Prerequisites
- Safety in the herd environment.
- Level 1 Yo-Yo Game skills.

Outcomes
- Horse focused more on you than the herd.
- Equal backwards and forwards. Both at no more than Phase 2-3.
- Building draw away from the herd by allowing your horse to rest away from the herd.

Steps

1. Position your horse so that he is facing you and play Friendly Game.

2. Back your horse to the end of your line, then allow him about 7 seconds to rest.

3. Bring him back to you and play Friendly Game. Repeat

5-7 times or until your horse is focused on you.

4. Using Yo-Yo Game, back your horse away from the herd and allow him to rest

Savvy Tips
• Remember your Phases to back your horse out: 1. Wiggle your finger (the rope and halter should not be moving). 2. Wiggle your wrist (this will wiggle the rope). 3. Wiggle your elbow (this will wiggle the snap on the halter). 4. Wiggle your shoulder (this will wiggle the halter).
• Remember to comb the rope with gradually increasing pressure when you draw your horse back towards you.

Troubleshooting
• *My horse will not keep his feet still for 7 seconds!*
That's ok, he may need to keep moving. So, only leave him out for 1 second, then bring him back (you can always increase the time he is away from you, later on).
• *My horse isn't backing straight.*
This means he isn't yet thinking backwards (his brain is still trying to come up with other answers – Sideways, moving HQ, etc.), keep playing the game until you get a straight back up.

Ways To Advance This Exercise
• Aim at and reward for straightness and effort. Have a goal in the back of your mind that when you ask with Phase 1 you would like your horse to flow backwards. A good visual is: think of a bubble floating in air, think how easy it is to move that bubble through the air by blowing in its direction. As you play Yo-Yo Game, keep this visualization in mind for how light your horse could go backwards.

7. Transitions On The Circle

Prerequisites
• Safety in the herd environment.
• Parelli Level 2 Circling Game and transitions on the circle.

Outcomes
• Horse focused more on you than the herd.
• Building draw away from the herd by allowing your horse to rest away from the herd.
• Teaching your horse to maintain his responsibilities.

Steps

1. Send your horse out on a circle next to the herd.

2. Now you are going to ask for transitions. If your horse likes to GO, you will focus on the downward transitions. If your horse likes to WHOA, you will focus on the upward transitions.
3. Start a pattern. Every half circle ask for a transition. For example, each time your horse circles closest to the herd, ask for trot. Each time your horse is furthest from the herd, ask for a walk. By doing this pattern you are also

helping your horse find comfort (going slower) away from the herd.

4. Repeat until your horse is tuning in to Phase 1-2, then allow him to rest on the side of the circle that is away from the herd.

Savvy Tips
• Use your Phases for upward transitions:
  1. Lead with your lead rope and turn in the direction your horse is traveling.
  2. Lift your stick.
  3. Swing your stick.
  4. Touch your horse with your stick.
• Use your Phases for downward transitions:
  1. Lower your energy and turn in the oppositve direction your horse is traveling.
  2. Lift your stick in front of your horse.
  3. Wiggle your stick in front of your horse.
  4. Wiggle the rope and stick until your horse makes a downward transition.

Troubleshooting
• *My horse ignores my rope wiggle to make a downward transition.*
  Go back to Yo-Yo Game and be sure he is responding. Also, keep wiggling until he at least slows down and then reward, this will build to a transition.
• *My horse is pulling me towards the herd.*
  This means he is still thinking about being in the herd. You may need to use a shorter rope. Stand in a power position, then be sure to reward him by bringing him in to you the moment he is not pulling towards the herd.

8. Zone 3 Mirror

Prerequisites
- Safety in the herd.
- Knowledge of the Parelli 'Stick To Me' game.
- Yo-Yo in Zone 3.

Outcomes
- Horse focused more on you than the herd.
- Building draw away from the herd by allowing your horse to rest away from the herd.
- Teaching your horse to follow your energy when you are in Zone 3.

Steps
1. Stand beside your horse and play Friendly Game until he is confident with you in that position.

2. Ask your horse to mirror your footsteps as you walk forward.

3. Ask your horse to stop with you and mirror your steps backwards.

4. Continue this pattern until your horse is tuned in and is able to match your steps for at least a few strides. Walk with him in this manner away from the herd and allow him to rest.

Savvy Tips
- Be sure your horse is walking with you. You want your first step to also be his first step.
- Use your Phases to get forwards with your Carrot Stick on his back. After he is moving, remember to go back to Friendly with the stick.
- Bring your stick up to Zone 1 to help keep your horse straight while backing.

Troubleshooting
- *My horse won't move forwards.*
  Use your Phases for Driving Game and be sure to reward the slightest try.
- *My horse keeps swinging his HQ away when I ask for backwards.*
  Often before your horse swings his HQ away he brings his nose in front of you – to stop this, bring your Carrot Stick forward to block Zone 1. Also, at the start, ask for only a few steps backwards. As your horse improves and you can control the direction, you will be able to ask for more and more steps.

Ways To Advance This Exercise
- As you advance your horse mirroring you, you can even add in changes of speed at the walk and trot. See if your horse can mirror three different speeds in each gait. Eventually you can take this to including very slow trot, almost trotting on the spot!

9. 1 Million Transitions

Prerequisites
• Level 1 Understanding and skills.
• Yo-Yo Game.
• Circling Game.

Outcomes
• Horse focused more on you than the herd.
• Building draw away from the herd by allowing your horse to rest away from the herd.
• Phase 2-3 responses when asking for transitions.

Steps
1. Stand near the herd but at least a rope's distance away. Send your horse in a circle.

2. Allow your horse to travel around the circle until he is maintaining gait, with you in neutral.
3. Add downward and upward transitions at least every half-circle.

4. Once your horse is focused on you, bring him in and walk

to the appropriate distance away from the herd, then allow him to rest.

Savvy Tips
- Remember your goal is to use the transitions to get your horse focused on you. If he is still distracted you may need to add transitions more often.
- Use your Phases for an upward transition:
  1. Life and energy up as you turn with horse, lift your lead rope arm to 'send' into upward transition.
  2. Lift your hand with the stick and string.
  3. Swing your stick.
  4. Touch your horse (touch your horse's "bubble" if you are too far away to actually touch the skin).
- Use your downward transition Phases:
  1. Bring your life and energy down as you turn against your horse's direction.
  2. Lift your stick in front of Zone 1 as you continue turning with him.
  3. As you keep the stick up in front of Zone 1, wiggle the stick.
  4. Continue wiggling the stick, now wiggle the rope as well until your horse makes the downward transition.

Troubleshooting
- *My horse speeds up when I ask for a downward transition.*
  Be sure your Carrot Stick is in front of your horse. You may need to go back to Yo-Yo Game to be sure your horse understands to yield back from rope wiggling.
- *My horse will not go into a trot/canter.*
  Bring him in closer to you so that you can be effective with your Phases. This way, Phase 4 will touch your horse. Also, be sure to reward him for the slightest try.

10. Connection Through Circling Changes

Prerequisites
- Be sure you are safe in the herd environment.
- Parelli Level 2 rope handling and On Line skills.

Outcomes
- Horse focused more on you than the herd.
- Building draw away from the herd by allowing your horse to rest away from the herd.
- Getting your horse to focus and learn the puzzle you have created. You want it to feel like he is figuring out the pattern.

Steps

1. Move to a safe distance from the herd (still close but so that your rope doesn't tangle with the other horses). Send your horse on the circle and allow him to maintain gait for 2-3 laps at trot or canter.

2. Ask for a change of direction then send in the new direction at the same gait.
3. Build a pattern, changing direction at the same time/point each time on the circle. (If your horse is impulsive change direction after half a lap, rather than after a whole lap).

4. When your horse is focused on you and the changes are happening more easily, disengage and bring him in to you. Walk with him and allow him to rest away from the herd.

Savvy Tips

- Remember to keep your change of direction body language clear and specific, so that it doesn't look like your "game over," or disengage, body language. Walking straight back, and straight back in, for the change of direction.
- After your horse changes direction, make your way back to the center of your circle.

Troubleshooting

- *My horse is coming too close to me on the change of direction.*
  This means that you need to be more effective with sending Zone 1 back out. You may need to go back to Driving Game in Zone 1 and 2.
- *My horse is ignoring me when I walk straight backwards.*
  After you have taken two steps back, begin wiggling the rope to interrupt your horse's pattern. As soon as he looks at you, softly send him in the new direction.

Ways To Advance This Exercise

- This can be a great exercise and the lightness you can get in the change of direction is only up to your imagination. While you are playing with these changes and building towards progression, think of your horse eventually responding from just your weight shifting back, without even needing to move your feet. You can build towards this by rewarding your horse for any response at a lighter Phase while playing this game.

11. Close Range Circling

Prerequisites
- Be sure you feel safe in the herd environment and that you are aware of the other horses.
- Level 1 understanding of Friendly and Driving Games.

Outcomes
- Horse focused more on you than the herd.
- Building draw away from the herd by allowing your horse to rest away from the herd.
- Your horse tuning in to just your lift and energy up while you are in Zone 3 (preparation for riding).

Steps

1. Use Friendly Game with your Carrot Stick on Zone 3 until your horse is accepting both the stick and you in Zone 3. If your horse gets worried you can always come back to Friendly Game.

2. Use your Phases to ask your horse to go forwards around you in a circle. Once he is moving allow the stick to simply rest on his back.

3. Play with transitions while he is circling you. See if you can get him in tune with your body language to bring his energy up and down.
4. Once he is in tune with your requests and looking to your leadership drive him away from the herd and rest.

Savvy Tips
- Once your horse is in motion, allow your stick to rest on his back (Friendly Game) while he is in motion
- Use your Phases when asking for upward transitions:
  1. Life and energy up and lift the rope forward.
  2. Lift the stick.
  3. Allow your stick to drop on his back.
  4. Use rhythmic pressure on Zone 3-4 until he moves.
- Remember your downward transition Phases:
  1. Lower your energy and lift the rope up.
  2. Begin to wiggle the rope.
  3. Bring your Carrot Stick forward in front of the drive line and tap it up and down on the ground.
  4. Wiggle the rope strongly and use Driving Game with the Carrot Stick in Zone 2-3.

Troubleshooting
- *My horse keeps stopping and looking at me.*
  Keep being patient, go back to Friendly Game in Zone 3 until your horse is relaxed. Ask for one step at a time and then reward, until your horse gets the idea.
- *My horse is running around me.*
  Spend more time playing Friendly Game and ask for only one step at a time on the circle.

12. Sideways Around Herd

Prerequisites
- Be sure you feel safe in the herd before playing with your horse in this environment.
- Sideways without a fence.

Outcomes
- Horse focused more on you than the herd.
- Building draw away from the herd by allowing your horse to rest away from the herd.
- Building a responsive Sideways (Phase 2-3), where your horse stops drifting forwards.

Steps
1. Warm your horse up with some FQ and HQ yields with a goal of lightness of response.

2. Using Driving Game send your horse Sideways.

3. If your horse drifts forward you can lift and wiggle the rope to remind him "by the way, don't go forward."

4. Each time your horse puts in some extra effort give him a little rest. Continue playing Sideways in both directions until your horse is focused on you and then allow him to rest away from the herd.

Savvy Tips

- Horses will naturally drift towards the herd – you can use this to your advantage. If your horse drifts backwards when you ask for Sideways then put the herd in front of him to help draw him forwards. If your horse drifts forwards during Sideways then put your horse's HQ on the herd side so that the natural draw will bring him backwards.
- Pick a focus over your horse's back so that you can keep a straight line.

Troubleshooting

- *My horse keeps going backwards.*
  Keep yourself on your "focus line" and use your skills to bring your horse forwards back to your focus line (like a circle send). By keeping yourself on your line you will give your horse a focus to come back to.
- *My horse runs forward and then turns to face me.*
  Use your rope wiggle up and down sooner to interrupt the forward. Be sure to stay on your line and if he goes too far forward, disengage, send him back to your line, disengage and start Sideways the same way again.

"If he's blinking, he's thinking,
if he's not, he's HOT."–Pat Parelli

13. Sideways From Porcupine

Prerequisites
• Be certain you are safe in the herd environment.
• Level 1 understanding of the Porcupine Game.

Outcomes
• Horse focused more on you than the herd.
• Building draw away from the herd by allowing your horse to rest away from the herd.
• Your horse yielding away from just your fingers pushing on the hair/skin. This is a great preparation for riding.

Steps
1. Move your horse a safe distance away from the herd, but still close enough that he isn't concerned. Using Porcupine Game yield your horse's FQ and HQ to warm him up for this exercise.

2. Now you are going to start asking for Sideways, at first use the same locations you did for yielding the FQ and HQ (Level 1 style), yield the FQ one step, then the HQ one step, then the FQ one step , then the HQ one step, etc.

3. As you continue this flow, begin moving your hands closer together to meet in Zone 3 (about the same place your leg would hang when you are riding).
4. As you begin to get steps with your hands both in the same position as your leg, reward with a little break. Continue this on both sides until your horse is asking you questions. Porcupine him Sideways away from the herd and allow him to rest.

Savvy Tips
• Remember your Phases for Porcupine Game:
Friendly first (rub).
1. Press the HAIR.
2. Press the SKIN.
3. Press the MUSCLE.
4. Press the BONE.
• Reward the slightest try. Even though you have a goal, be sure you are rewarding your horse along your way to the goal, so that he can learn what you are teaching.

Troubleshooting
• *My horse is not moving!*
Go through your Phases for Porcupine and once you get to "bone" hold it while you apply some Driving Game pressure, this should help to "unlock" your horse's feet.
• *My horse won't go Sideways.*
Remember that the two parts your horse needs to move for Sideways is the FQ and the HQ. As long as you are able to yield these you have something to "work" with. If your horse gets stuck with the Sideways request, go back to the exaggeration of just HQ and/or just FQ until he feels successful, and then try again. Reward for the slightest try.

14. Over Or Between

Prerequisites
• Safety in the herd environment.
• Level 1 Squeeze Game skills.

Outcomes
• Horse focused more on you than the herd.
• Building draw away from the herd by allowing your horse to rest away from the herd.
• By building your horse's confidence in tight spaces you will look for him to become more relaxed and willing.

Steps

1. Choose an "obstacle" (a flower, the fence, a log/stick, a pile of poop), and play Squeeze Game with it.

2. After you've Squeezed your horse through a few times now "Raise The Baar," ask your horse to go straighter for longer, maybe 4-6' more before they turn and face you.

3. Once this is going well, "Raise The Baar" again by being particular that he stops after he turns and faces, you want to be able to ask him to disengage and stop, not always come in to you.

4. When your horse is responsive and focused on you, drive him away (using Driving Game to move him) from the herd and allow him to rest.

Savvy Tips

• Have a clear release, when your horse is in the Squeeze you need to be in neutral. Make sure you aren't holding your arms up, in a continuous Phase 2. Follow the Phases of Squeeze Game:

1. Send.

2. ALLOW.

3. Turn, face, and WAIT.

• If there is a dominant horse in the herd, be aware of where that horse is so that he doesn't get the opportunity to drive your horse while you are playing.

Troubleshooting

• *My horse won't go straight after the Squeeze.*

Drive Zone 1 after the Squeeze. If your horse ignores your request or pushes into it you may need to go back to Driving Game on the FQ and re-establish some respect.

• *My horse won't Squeeze in between me and the fence.*

Take a few steps back away from the fence so that your horse has more room, open the door and make the puzzle easier, so that your horse can feel successful.

15. Sideways And Squeeze Combo

Prerequisites
- Be sure you feel safe and confident in a herd environment.
- Level 1-2 Sideways and Squeeze Game skills.
- A paddock with a safe and appropriate fence for you and your horse to drive Sideways along.

Outcomes
- Horse focused more on you than the herd.
- Building draw away from the herd by allowing your horse to rest away from the herd.
- Creating a flow from Sideways to Squeeze Game where your feet are moving in a rhythm.

Steps

1. Choose an appropriate and safe fence in your horse's paddock and play Sideways Game down the fence.

2. Now walk a few steps away from the fence and invite your horse to Squeeze in between you and the fence, then ask him to turn and face.

3. Walk back to the fence and send your horse Sideways in the new direction, repeat.

4. Keep this pattern going in a flow until your horse is really focused on you and then take him away from the herd and allow him to rest for about 5 minutes (less if he needs to move his feet again).

Savvy Tips

• Have a clear picture of what you're asking your horse to do. This is a great time to ask friends at the barn to be your "conga horse" and allow you to simulate with them.

• Keep the flow going, keep a rhythm in your head that you march out in your feet.

• When asking for Sideways stay close to the fence. If you drift away from the fence it is inviting your horse to Squeeze in between you and the fence.

Troubleshooting

• *My horse backs up when I ask for Sideways.*
  Most importantly keep your feet close to the fence, then use your stick and string to "reach out" and do Driving Game, however far away he is. If you can't reach him with your stick and string just aim your energy towards the Zone that needs to move, and release for the slightest try.

• *My horse is running through the Squeeze.*
  Back up another step or two away from the fence so that he has more room and doesn't feel as claustrophobic. This may help him relax and walk through. Also, be sure you are relaxed and that your stick and string are down so that you are not putting additional pressure on him.

Ways To Advance This Exercise

• As you look at bringing your horsemanship to the next level, keep in mind that this can be a fun game to play at Liberty. If you play On Line with that in mind it will help you become more aware of all the moments you use your rope (these are moments where your horse may have left you if you were at Liberty).

"Set it up and WAIT."

16. Circling To Sideways

Prerequisites
- Safety in the herd.
- Fence that is appropriate and safe for Sideways Game.
- Level 2 skills in Sideways and Circling.
- 22-foot line skills will make this exercise easier.

Outcomes
- Horse focused more on you than the herd.
- Building draw away from the herd by allowing your horse to rest away from the herd.
- To create flow between Circle and Sideways and help your horse tune in to you by creating some variety to how you put the games together.

Steps
1. At a safe distance away from the herd play Circling Game with some changes of direction and/or transitions to get your horse focused on you.

2. Now as your horse circles, walk your feet towards the fence.

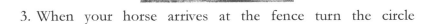

3. When your horse arrives at the fence turn the circle

energy into Sideways (it's better to start this at walk or trot so that your horse isn't as likely to think about jumping the fence).

4. Continue Sideways down the fence until he is traveling with a flow, then walk away from the fence, invite your horse to Squeeze between you and the fence, and carry on in a circle around you. Repeat until he is focused on you and then take your circle away from the herd to rest.

Savvy Tips
- Keep your feet flowing, you are asking your horse to complete these maneuvers in a flow so it is important the leader (you) keeps a flow as well.
- Begin slowly, you can always add more speed as you go, but in the beginning it can be easier to go slow and give yourself more time to think.

Troubleshooting
- *My horse stops at the fence and just looks at me.*
  Give him a smile and then drive Zone 1-2 until he is perpendicular to the fence, then begin Sideways. If he seems to get worried you may need to spend some time playing Friendly Game once he is perpendicular to the fence.

Well Done Completing This Section!

You have taken huge steps in improving your relationship with your horse and building a partnership your horse is glad to be a part of!

A Reminder Of Where To Go From Here

Now that you have completed the exercises in this section you may find it useful to use additional sections and adjust the exercises to fit your situation. These sections will review some of the information you just covered and they will give you additional tools and perspectives for continuing to build your relationship.

Another option is to take what you have learned from this section and go straight to the exercises in the Riding section, keeping track of your program on the Partner Progress Pages.

Last, read over the Emergency Strategy section so that you will be better prepared for unforeseen situations if they arise.

At any time you feel you need a little "refresher," have quick read back over the theory section as a reminder to look at things from your horse's perspective.

"Slow and right, beats fast and wrong."

SECTION 2

Horses Kept In
A Stall
Or Barn

Strategies for building confidence in your
horse, when separating them from the herd,
in the barn, and their stall.
These techniques will be most relevant for
horses that are kept in a barn. In addition, you can use
most of the exercises from "Horses Kept In Pairs."

Horsenality Filter: Horse In Barn/Stall

As you progress through the following section you may find the Horsenality filter below useful to help tailor each exercise to fit your individual horse.

LB Extrovert

- Keep your session active – this horse needs to move his feet to stay interested in the session.
- If you are skilled with your ropes, longer lines will be more helpful with this horse when you move outside the barn.
- The exercises that fit this Horsenality most specifically are: 18, 21, 23-25.

RB Extrovert

- Consistency and patterns are the key with this horse.
- Match his energy plus 4 ounces, without becoming predatory.
- Longer lines will allow this horse to drift as you move out of the barn.
- The exercises that fit this Horsenality most specifically are: 18, 21, 23-25.

LB Introvert

- Be ready to drive Zone 1 effectively.
- Allow him time to think.
- Prepare to reward the slightest try.
- Less is more with this Horsenality.
- All of the exercises in this section are suited to this horse.

RB Introvert

- Be ready to WAIT for a long time between tasks until he can think.
- Use a clear but light Phase 1 for a long time before getting stronger.
- Use patterns and consistency to build confidence and trust in you.
- All of the exercises in this section are suited to this horse.

Safety Reminders

Be aware of other horses that may have their heads out of stalls. Be sure the footing is safe in the area you are asking your horse to travel. Be sure your horse doesn't slip on the center aisle (particularly if he has shoes on and he is traveling on a cement aisle).

Catching Game Tips For Inside Your Stall

In this environment you can play the "classic" catching game. You may even be able to stand at the stall door and play (stalls are such tight spaces that often you can apply PLENTY of pressure to motivate your horse without even being in the stall). Remember, start soft, you can always increase the pressure if your horse doesn't respond.

Rewards Away From The Barn

Rest, scratches, food, water/molasses water, grass, rolling.

Distance Away From Stall For Reward

Start by rewarding in the stall, move to rewarding in the aisle, right outside barn, 22 feet away from barn, 45 feet away from barn, in arena, on other side of property, etc.

Level Recommendations

Adjust the exercise to fit your savvy level: Level 1 – 12-foot line, Level 2 – 22-foot line, Level 3-4 – 45-foot line.

Helpful References

Parelli Zones Of The Horse for reference as you read through the following section.

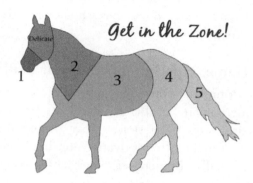

Seven Games Summary And Reminders

Principle Games

1. Friendly Game: This game is the Confidence Game – to help your horse gain confidence in people, places, changes and things. While playing this game you will use:

• *Approach and Retreat*   • *Rhythm*.

2. Porcupine Game: This game is focused around the concept of teaching your horse to *Follow a Feel*.

3. Driving Game: This game is about getting your horse to *Follow a Suggestion*.

Purpose Games

4. Yo-Yo Game: The to and fro game. By using this game you help your horse balance *Backwards and Forwards*.

5. Circling Game: The purpose of circling to help your horse learn his *Responsibilities*.

6. Sideways Game: This game is all about *Lateral Movements*.

7. Squeeze Game: Also known as the *Matador Game*. This game is about *Shortening Your Horse's Flight Line* and helping them build confidence in situations they perceive as a Squeeze or as claustrophobic.

17. Follow A Feel,
You Choose The Zone

Prerequisites
• Safety in your stall with your horse.
• Safety around your horse while rubbing them with your hands.

Outcomes
• Rewarding for Phase 1 and 2 responses (hair, skin).
• Teaching your horse how to yield off of pressure in different zones.
• Causing your horse to focus more on you.

Steps
1. Play Friendly Game first with the area of your horse you will Porcupine (ex. If you are going to ask him to move from pressure on his chin, rub this area first until he accepts your Friendly Game).

2. Using the Phases of Porcupine ask him to move off of a steady feel.

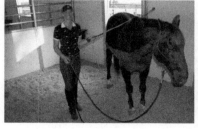

3. Each time he gives you an improvement/try reward with a little rest and rub.
4. If possible time your release so that your rewards occur when his nose is pointed away from his stall/buddy. Continue these games using different areas: chin, ear, halter, etc., until he is focused on you, then reward him at the appropriate distance from his comfort.

Savvy Tips
- Use the Four Phases of Porcupine:
  - Press the HAIR, Press the SKIN, Press the MUSCLE, Press the BONE.
- Be sure to reward when your horse moves; you can go back to Friendly Game to reward in the beginning. As you advance and start asking for more steps in a flow, reward one step by going back to Phase 1, repeat this process until your horse is yielding off of Phase 1.

Troubleshooting
- *My horse won't move!*
  Be aware of when you release, developing lightness is all about timing. If you take the pressure away when your horse is holding still you have just taught him that in order to get release he needs to hold still. To help change this pattern, look for the slightest change (a weight shift, or an ear heading in the direction you are asking) and reward. Soon you will get a step.
- *My horse doesn't move until I get to Phase 4 EVERY time!*
  First, be sure you are starting at Phase 1 and going through your Phases each time. Second, you can use Driving Game to support Porcupine. To do this keep the Porcupine pressure on and add rhythmic pressure in Phases with your other hand/stick until he moves, and then reward. Soon your horse will associate the steady pressure with movement and release.

18. Circling In Stall

Prerequisites
- Safety in the stall with your horse.
- Level 1 On Line skills.

Outcomes
- Causing your horse to become more focused on you by moving his feet on a circle when he becomes distracted.
- Getting your horse tuned in to your energy through transitions. When tuned in he should respond at Phase 2-3.

Steps
1. While remaining in the controlled space of your stall you can introduce circles. After haltering your horse in the stall send your horse around you in a circle. Be sure he is not worried in the tight space and you are safe being in the stall with him.

 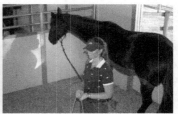

2. After 1-3 laps draw him back, repeat in other direction.
3. If you both feel up to it you can even add in transitions, walk to halt and halt to walk.

4. Continue this pattern until your horse is focused on you. Each time you bring him in, allow him to find comfort with you. After 5-7 repetitions draw him to you and take him out of the stall to rest.

Savvy Tips
• Remember your Phases to send: 1. Lead your horse with the lead rope. 2. Lift the Carrot Stick. 3. Swing the Carrot Stick. 4. Touch your horse with the end of the stick.
• Be sure you aren't putting too much pressure on your horse while he is in the stall, this is a tight space and can be claustrophobic for horses.
• The goal is for your horse to find release and comfort with you so that you create more draw to YOU!

Troubleshooting
• *My horse gets panicked in the stall when I try to circle him.*
This may be too tight of a space for your horse, you might try doing the close range Circling Game from Zone 3. This could help your horse stay more connected and not get so lost and confused.
• *My horse won't move, he just looks bored and no matter how hard I use my stick he only goes one step.*
There are two likely reasons here: 1. He is afraid and "can't" move; or 2. He is dominant and "won't" move. Either way it may help you to go back to the close range Circling from Zone 3 exercise. Be sure to reward for the slightest try and give him a little rub when he offers one step. Start again at Phase 1 and reward the slightest try each time. Soon his feet should "free up."

Ways To Advance This Exercise
• If you are having a lot of fun playing this game you can start to include more transitions, more often, and include backwards and changes of directions (by using "yielding the HQ until you get the other eye," and allowing this to flow into forwards).

19. Sideways Point To Point In Stall

Prerequisites
• Safety while in the stall with your horse.
• Level 1 Sideways skills.

Outcomes
• Causing your horse to become more focused on you by giving him somewhere to go and allowing him to rest when he gets there.
• Building a pattern of purpose when you ask your horse to do something (the purpose in this case is rest).

Steps
1. Point to point is a great exercise to motivate and provide purpose to our horses. While still in the stall pick a focus and ask your horse to go Sideways to that point.

2. When you get there allow him to rest for a moment then switch sides and pick a new point, drive him Sideways the other way to the new point.
3. Repeat this exercise until he is focused on you and the Sideways has improved.

4. To finish the session drive your horse from Zone 3 out of the stall/barn and allow him to rest, away from his stall.

Savvy Tips

• If you have a horse that is still a little over reactive to your Driving Game you can do this same exercise with Porcupine Game. Often Porcupine Game is more reassuring for this type of horse because you are staying more in contact with them. (You can refer back to Exercise 18 for more details.)

Troubleshooting

• *My horse won't stay at the wall when I go up to rub him, he walks forward.*

This is most likely a Friendly/Squeeze Game issue and has to do with him not feeling confident in the Squeeze between you and the wall. Take your time and build his confidence, be aware of his threshold and respect the space he feels he needs. Continue to take the opportunities to play Friendly Game in this zone whenever you can, to build his confidence and understanding.

Ways To Advance This Exercise

• To mix this up you can pick different zones of your horse to reach the point. For example, if you have a horse that continues to lag their HQ on Sideways, you may choose the HQ to be the point that has to reach your focus before allowing your horse to rest.

20. Sideways Towards With Porcupine On The Rope

Prerequisites
- Level 3 On Line development and understanding with your horse, particularly with Porcupine.
- Level 3 rope handling, feel, and timing.

Outcomes
- To help your horse understand how to yield from pressure in all zones, rather than follow his nature and push into the pressure.
- Get your horse more focused on you by giving him many unique puzzles to solve.

Steps

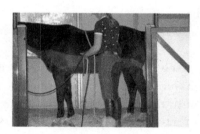

1. Play Friendly Game with the 22-foot rope around your horse's Zone 3 until he is calm and not bothered.

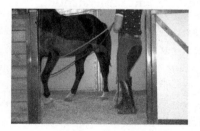

2. Holding both ends of the rope with it wrapped around Zone 3, use your Phases of Porcupine and ask your horse to yield towards you.

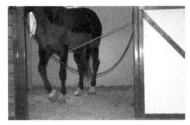

3. Reward any try, even if he just shifts his weight (this can be a hard puzzle for horses to solve and you want to take your time and offer a good feel and great experience).
4. As your horse begins to understand and becomes focused on you, bring him away from the herd to allow him to rest/eat.

Savvy Tips

- Go slow, allow you and your horse time to think. This is a task that will go better when you take more time, you don't want to rush your horse.
- The goal behind asking your horse to yield in this manner is to develop his depth and understanding of Porcupine. By doing this you are helping him to see you as a good leader and developing your communication language. As a result, he will become more interested in your leadership.

Troubleshooting

- *My horse pushes into the rope and moves away from me.*
  He may need you to break the exercise down in smaller chunks to help him learn. If he moves into the pressure, you can go to the other side of your horse and reestablish Porcupine off your hand in Zone 3 for Sideways. Once this is soft and he understands, switch sides and try again. Repeat until he can "bridge" the gap.
- *My horse is bucking!*
  Abort mission! If he is bucking, either the pressure was applied too quickly or he does not yet have the understanding and positive response to steady pressure needed to play this game successfully.

21. Backwards Responsibility

Prerequisites
• Level 2+.

Outcomes
• To teach your horse a new way to maintain responsibility.
• To create more draw towards you by becoming more interesting than everything else around your horse.
• Resting when your horse's mind is focused away from his stall/buddy so that he builds more draw to you.

Steps

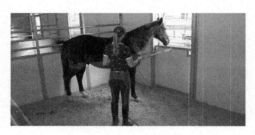

1. Starting in your horse's stall, you are going to ask him to maintain gait backwards in a circle around you. Start by being in the center of your stall with your horse in a Driving from Zone 3 position.

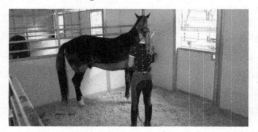

2. Ask your horse to back by wiggling the rope. If he swings his HQ away, bring his nose towards you using your stick to block Zone 1 and drive it away so that he is in position to back again.

3. Ask him to back by going through your Phases. Each time he backs start back at Phase 1 (just your energy) and see if he will take at least one more step. When he does, give him a big reward and scratches.

4. Back him out of the stall and allow him to rest away from the stall/barn.

Savvy Tips

• As you advance this exercise you can ask your horse to maintain his responsibility of backing around you for a longer and longer time. Keep in mind that he needs to be able to read your body language if he should stop or keep backing. To help him with this, be sure when you are asking for backing that you have some energy in your body to promote energy in his body.

Troubleshooting

• *My horse won't keep backing!*

At this stage that is okay, this can be something that takes horses a while to understand. Be patient and remember how long it took before your horse would maintain gait around you on the circle at walk, trot or canter? This may take time as well, stick with it and keep going through your Phases and giving your horse the chance to respond.

22. Yielding Sideways Away From Steady Pressure

Prerequisites
• Level 1 understanding of Porcupine Game.
• Safety when at close range with your horse, rubbing and playing Porcupine.

Outcomes
• Rewarding for Phase 1 and 2 responses (hair, skin).
• Teaching your horse how to yield off of pressure with the possibility of building towards riding.
• Causing your horse to focus more on you.

Steps

1. You can begin this exercise in your stall or in the aisle. Warm your horse up with Porcupine, moving the FQ and HQ.

2. Begin to bring your hands closer to the front of Zone 3 (where your leg hangs when you ride). Ask for one step with the HQ then one step with the FQ.

3. Continue this pattern until there is less and less time between the steps, so that it starts to look and feel like your horse is flowing Sideways.

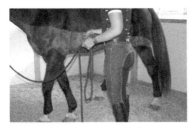

4. Keep repeating the pattern until you are able to ask for the Sideways response with just one hand, right where your leg will hang when you are riding. Finish by allowing your horse to rest away from his buddy, gradually increasing the distance, starting at a few feet away.

Savvy Tips
- Use the Four Phases of Porcupine: Press the HAIR, Press the SKIN, Press the MUSCLE, Press the BONE.
- If your horse starts to get confused, remember you have the tools to isolate the parts of Sideways and fix it (move the HQ one step, move the FQ one step). Just slow things down and help your horse by separating, isolating and then recombining.
- As you get the feel for this exercise you can use a game of "point to point" to improve your horse's response. Choose two points and yield your horse Sideways back and forth between these points. Allow him to rest at each point.

Troubleshooting
- *My horse is not moving!*
  Use the rhythm of Driving Game to support the steady pressure of Porcupine Game.
- *My horse is just walking forwards.*
  You can use your rope and "lift to stop the drift." Give him a little upward bump with the rope on the halter to help stop the forward drift.

23. "Touch it"

Prerequisites
• Level 1 skills Driving from Zone 3.

Outcomes
• Teaching your horse to follow your focus.
• Helping your horse learn that there is something good in what you are asking him to do (by allowing him to rest when he gets to the destination).
• Causing your horse to focus more on you.

Steps

1. While in your stall pick an object (you could bring one in with you, like a cone or cavaletti block). From Zone 3 drive your horse to the object. When they get there, allow them to rest/give them a scratch.
2. Pick your next object/point, wait about 7 seconds and then drive them to that object.

3. Continue this game including areas in the aisle (not other horses), and outside the barn (once outside you can drive

from grass patch to grass patch).

4. As you play, be aware that you can switch sides and this will provide a new learning opportunity for both you and your horse.

Savvy Tips

- In the beginning, pick objects that will help you stop your horse (bigger things/things on a wall/fence), this way your horse can't walk over the object without ever realizing it is there.
- Be specific about your horse putting his Zone 1 on the object you picked.
- Remember to switch sides and practice just as much or more on the right side of your horse.

Troubleshooting

- *My horse keeps turning in front of me and away from my object.*
  Use your Carrot Stick and bring it forwards to block Zone 1 from turning. You may be able to just bring the stick forward and rhythmically "tap" it in the air while pointed at your object. This motion may be enough to keep your horse's nose from turning. If not, go to the isolation of Driving the FQ until your horse is responding at a light Phase, then go back to the exercise.
- *My horse won't let me stay in Zone 3.*
  Go back to Friendly Game in Zone 3 until your horse feels confident with you "hanging out" in Zone 3. Now, go back to Driving Game in Zone 3 and at each arrival point give your horse a lot of Friendly Game by "hanging out" beside him.

24. Approach and Retreat

Prerequisites
• Understanding of Level 1 Squeeze Game.

Outcomes
• Building confidence leaving the stall.
• Noticing where your horse's discomfort starts, so that you know where to start to build his confidence.
• Causing your horse to focus more on you.

Steps
1. Starting with the stall door open, position yourself on the outside of the stall, beside the wall (so that you are in a safe position and cannot get squished as your horse walks in and out of the stall). You will be preparing to play Squeeze Game.

2. Play the Squeeze Game and ask your horse to come out of his stall, turn, face, and wait.

3. Allow him to wait until he is licking and chewing and/or showing signs of relaxation.

4. Send him in his stall, turn, face, and wait just a moment, then send him out again. Allow him time to rest when he is outside of his stall. Repeat this process until it's easier to send him out of his stall than to send him in the stall, and then give him a big break away from his stall.

Savvy Tips

• Some horses, particularly introverts, can have anxiety from just leaving the comfort of their stalls. This is an important thing to notice and help your horse find comfort outside the stall even at this very early stage.
• Taking the time it takes here will save you time in the long run. Trust is so important, particularly for Right Brained Introverts. By not pushing him past his comfort/learning zones you will build more trust with this horse.

Troubleshooting

• *My horse won't leave his stall.*
Well done recognizing his inability or unwillingness to leave. The key here is to cause it to be the horse's idea to leave. So, go in the stall and play some of the Games, ex. Driving from Zone 3 around the stall, Circling in the stall, Driving HQ and FQ in the stall. Now offer your horse the opportunity to leave the stall and rest on the outside. Repeat this process until your horse is willing and confident to leave the stall.

"Take the time it takes this time,
so it takes less time next time."

25. Backwards Through And Out

Prerequisites
• Level 1 Driving Game backwards in Zone 1.

Outcomes
• Responsive backwards with confidence. This will result in a low Phase of request, and rhythm while backing.
• More focus on you by giving your horse something to focus on, in this case backing to a location.

Steps
1. Using your Carrot Stick in Zone 1, drive your horse backwards out of the stall.

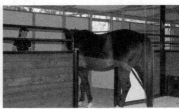

2. Each time your horse backs up with a little more effort give him a 5-7 second break (longer if needed), then pick a point to aim for while backing, and back him to that point.
3. Continue this pattern, making a serpentine-like shape down the aisle.
4. Once you are outside of the barn, continue backing in patterns (ex. Figure 8) until he is focused on you, then give him his reward at the appropriate distance away from the stall/barn.

Savvy Tips

- Remember to use your Driving Game Phases in Zone 1: 1. Lift your energy. 2. Tap the stick on the ground. 3. Begin to move towards your horse. 4. Allow the stick to "touch" your horse as you continue to tap.
- Although your goal may be to get all the way out of the barn, be sure to give your horse small rewards for a good try on the way.
- Keep a strong and clear focus on where you are backing to.

Troubleshooting

- *My horse will not back out of the stall.*
  The stall door can be an uncomfortable Squeeze for your horse. To help build your horse's confidence, use the Squeeze Game: Allow him to go in and out a few times. Next, using Yo-Yo ask him to stop when he is only partially through the Squeeze, and back out. Continue this, gradually increasing the amount of your horse that backs through the space until he is comfortable with the Squeeze, then try the exercise again.
- *After my horse gets outside he gets worried about his stall/ herd/ buddy.*
  This means in this moment we have stretched his comfort/ learning zone a little too far. Just back him back into the barn and allow him to rest where he feels comfortable, then start again. Be aware that you need to only "push" him to the edge of his learning zone but not through it. You can refer back to the theory section and the chart on comfort zone.

26. Drive HQ/FQ, Then Drive From Zone 3

Prerequisites
• Level 2 On Line skills.   .

Outcomes
• To have your horse tune in to your intention and follow your focus. Seen when he is able to move in a flow from HQ/FQ yielding to Zone 3 Driving without getting worried.
• To create a horse that is more focused on you and has less reason to think about his buddy/stall.

Steps

1. Start in your stall by Driving the HQ until your horse offers the other eye (refer to Exercise #5 for specific directions on this exercise), drive the FQ until your horse's HQ are pointed towards the open door, rub.

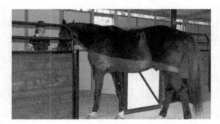

2. Wiggle the rope to back your horse out of the stall using Yo-Yo Game.

3. With your horse on the outside of the stall drive from Zone 3 out of the barn.

4. Play a combination of close range Circling and Driving from Zone 3 until you are at your rest location, then give your horse a big break/reward.

Savvy Tips
• The focus for this exercise is to keep the flow and rhythm going. Each piece doesn't need to be perfect, you are just trying to flow from one thing to the next.
• Keeping a focus and planning on the next thing you will be asking your horse to do will help offer him the leadership he needs to trust and respect you.

Troubleshooting
• *My horse will not back out of his stall.*
You may need to go back to a few Squeeze Games in and out of the stall until he is confident. Then ask him to stop part-way through, pause, and then ask him to back out. Repeat this, slowly backing more and more of your horse through the Squeeze until he is confident.

Ways To Advance This Exercise
• While building confidence and then more variety you can add more and more games to your Driving from Zone 3 play. As an example you may choose to add a repetition of Squeeze Game at a log or ditch. You could add in a few Yo-Yo Games from Zone 3, or even a close range circle or two.

27. Touch It With Foot/Nose/Tail

Prerequisites
• Level 2 Driving Game.
• You have successfully played traditional "Touch It" with your horse, touching objects with Zone 1.

Outcomes
• Begin to expand your relationship and communication with your horse by creating new puzzles.
• Catching your horse's mind so that he will become more focused on you.

Steps
1. Now that you have played Touch It in the previous exercise we are ready to bring things up to the next level by playing touch it with other zones! Pick a Zone/point on your horse, for example: foot, nose, tail, etc.

2. Pick a focus. To start with, pick something easy, for example if you choose your horse's right front foot then choose a cone. See if you can get your horse to place his right front foot on the cone.

3. When he does, give him a long rest/scratch and then pick a new point that will be safe for his right front foot to touch.
4. Once this is going well you can choose another part of his body, like his tail, and see how many things you can ask him to put his tail on (now you will need to add backwards to your Zone 3 Driving).

Savvy Tips

- As you are playing with these exercises keep in mind that you are trying to work your way through the exercise successfully, but the overall goal is to improve the leadership and relationship you have with your horse. You want him to want to be with you, and to feel confident away from the herd when he is with you.
- As you begin picking new parts of your horse, be patient with him, he is learning what you are asking. We have just changed the "rules" of the game. Before you were asking him to "touch it" with Zone 1; now that you have picked a new object and a new zone, it will take him a minute to figure out the new guidelines of the game.

Troubleshooting

- *My horse will not put his foot on the object.*
  Make sure he is not afraid of the object. If he is, you can either choose a different object or play some Squeeze Game and Friendly Game with the object until he becomes more confident. Next, be sure he can see the object. Sometimes picking bigger objects is easier. Also, as a leader, keep in mind that he needs you to accept a little try. As soon as he is one inch closer, or begins to *think* about the object, release. Like a game of "You're getting warmer."

28. Explore The Area From Zone 3

Prerequisites
• Level 1 Driving Game skills.
• Exercise 19.

Outcomes
• Building confidence in and around the stall and barn.
• Noticing where your horse's discomfort starts, so you can be respectful of their comfort zone.
• Causing your horse to focus more on you.

Steps
1. Make sure your horse is confident with you in Zone 3 on both sides and begin Driving from Zone 3 in your stall with the door open.

2. Once you can direct your horse to different points around your stall, begin to add in points in the aisle way.

3. Each time you arrive at a point, allow your horse to rest and play some Friendly Game while you wait.

4. Continue playing this game until you can drive your horse anywhere in the barn with confidence. Allow him to take a long rest/give him a big reward when he is farthest away from his stall/buddy.

Savvy Tips

- Choose points that are close to start with, think 12-22 feet away so that your horse learns the game and begins to realize there is something "good" (something important to your horse, ex. rest, scratches, food, etc.) in what you are asking him to do.
- Be sure to play this game from both sides of your horse.

Troubleshooting

- *My horse will not stop moving his feet when I get to the "point" and try to let him rest.*
  He may not be ready to stop yet. This means you need to give him some exercises where he can move his feet so you can create a situation where it is his idea to stop moving.

Ways To Advance This Exercise

- As you explore new areas, see if you can allow your horse to get there farther and farther ahead of you. By doing this you will set your focus, get your horse headed towards it, and then "hang back" a little. This can help build your horse's self confidence and trust in your leadership at greater distances.

"Do it for the horse, not to the horse."

29. Close Range Circling And Zone 3 Driving

Prerequisites
- Level 1+ Driving Game skills.
- You have already completed the previous Driving from Zone 3 exercise.

Outcomes
- Rewarding for responsiveness to your body language (Phase 1 and 2), showing that your horse is focused more on you.
- Helping your horse learn to tune in to and read your body language.

Steps
1. Begin in the same position used for Zone 3 Driving. You will be using the same Phases to ask your horse forward, but now you will keep your feet still.

2. As your horse moves forward, rotate around in a circle with him. You will be asking your horse to circle you while you keep the Carrot Stick on his back (in neutral).
3. Once this is going smoothly, pick a focus and go from the circle in a straight line to your focus. Once you get there rest, repeat.
4. Repeat this pattern as you play approach and retreat, moving closer and farther away from the stall. You can

go up and down the aisle, in and out of the barn/arena. Continue the pattern until your horse is focused on you and then drive him to a spot away from his herd/stall and allow him to rest/give him a reward.

Savvy Tips
- This is a great exercise for the horse that wants to keep moving his feet. It allows you to adjust and add a circle or more at any point while you are heading to an object.
- Play this from both sides of your horse.
- When your horse is going forwards be sure to allow your stick to come to neutral and rest on your horse's back so that you are not continuing to drive him once he is in motion.

Troubleshooting
- *My horse gets scared and/or rushes forward. The longer we circle the faster he goes!*
  Be sure your stick is resting on his back and not bouncing once he is going fast and has become emotional. You will need to remove your stick so that it doesn't bounce. Also, be sure he is confident with you standing in Zone 3 and rubbing him with your stick before adding motion. Last, if he gets worried only on the circle but is fine in the Driving from Zone 3 exercise, then only add ½ circles, then build to ¾ circles then full, then 1 ½, etc.
- *My horse won't go to my focus after the circle, he just keeps circling.*
  After changing your focus and aiming your focus at the new object you may need to lift your stick and drive Zone 1 so that he can't keep turning in front of you.

30. Sideways Point To Point In Aisle

Prerequisites
• Safe barn aisle.
• Level 1 Sideways skills.

Outcomes
• Create a more responsive Sideways. As a result you will get Phase 2-3 responses.
• Get your horse more focused on you. Each time he becomes distracted you can choose a new point and move his feet Sideways to that point.

Steps
1. Now that your horse is happy and confident out of his stall you can play Sideways up and down the aisle (or side to side in the aisle, depending on the size of your barn). As long as the stalled horses will not be bothered you can use the stalls as the "wall" for Sideways.

2. Ask your horse to travel Sideways down the barn aisle. When you reach the end, if your horse is confident, you can drive him Sideways outside and allow him to rest on the outside of the barn. If he is not yet ready to leave the aisle, switch sides and drive him Sideways back up the aisle.
3. Repeat this process until your horse is confident and traveling Sideways smoothly. Whenever possible, as you give

"mini releases," you will try to time these to when your horse is away from his buddy/stall in the barn.

4. After he is focused on you and responding willingly, give him a big reward on the outside of the barn.

Savvy Tips
- Remember to drive whatever zone is lagging. If your horse is in the habit of lagging with the HQ then make a point of allowing him to rest when he finally puts in more effort with the HQ. Also, be sure you aren't walking faster than your horse can go Sideways. At this stage it may help your horse's HQ to catch up by slowing your feet down.
- As you transition from Sideways to a stand still, be sure to bring your life and energy down so that your horse knows the game has changed.

Troubleshooting
- *My horse won't move.*
  Begin by breaking down the elements to Sideways. First we just need one step at a time. Ask for one step with the FQ by Driving Zone 1, then rub. Ask for one step with the HQ by Driving Zone 4, when he moves, rub. Repeat this about 7 times then give him a long break. Now start again with one step at a time and stop when he starts to flow, another long break. Now, begin to shorten the rest/rub time between each ask, just for 2-3 steps, then give a long break. Keep building the pattern this way and in no time your horse will figure out the pattern.

31. Squeeze To Sideways Down Aisle

Prerequisites
• Safe footing in the barn aisle.
• Level 1+ Sideways and Squeeze Game skills.

Outcomes
• Flowing going from Sideways to Squeeze.
• Having your horse more focused on you by providing him something to do with his feet and offering him rest when he is ready.
• Getting your horse more focused on you and less focused on the barn/stall/buddy/herd.

Steps
1. Begin by asking your horse to go Sideways down the rail/stall wall.

2. Once your horse is flowing Sideways, step your feet back away from the wall and ask them to Squeeze between you and the wall, disengage.

3. When your horse has two eyes on you, walk your feet back to the wall and drive your horse's Zone 1 so that he

is going Sideways in the opposite direction.

4. After Sideways is flowing in the new direction step away from the wall, Squeeze him through and repeat the process from step 3. Do this 5-7 times until it flows a little better and your horse is focused on you, then take him out of the barn to rest.

Savvy Tips

• This exercise flows better if you can maintain a rhythm and focus. You may want to try the "foot work" a few times without your horse so that it flows better when you have your horse.

• This is a great way to get your horse thinking about where his feet are, as well as focused on your communication. Just remember that even if it doesn't go well you can always bring your horse in to you and start over. They are most likely learning a new skill as well.

Troubleshooting

• *My horse keeps walking backwards away from the rail when I ask him to go Sideways.*
This is a common option horses try when playing Sideways. First, keep your feet next to the rail, even if you have to allow some rope to drift/slip. Also, allow your savvy string and Carrot Stick to reach out and touch your horse, or if you can't reach him then touch his bubble with your stick and string. Continue the rhythmic pressure until he comes back to the wall, then give him a little break. You may have to do this several times before he realizes there is no rest away from the wall.

32. Squeeze Game In And Out Of Barn

Prerequisites
- It is important to have safe aisle footing so that your horse won't slip while playing Squeeze Game.
- Your horse needs to be confident squeezing in and out of the stall and playing games up and down the aisle.

Outcomes
- Approach and retreat leaving the comfort zone.
- Helping your horse to become more focused on you. As a result they will be less focused on their buddy horse/barn.

Steps

1. Once your horse is confident squeezing in and out of his stall and you have played up and down the aisle. Now set yourself up to play Squeeze Game in and out of the barn. Pick a space where your horse won't be able to squish you if he rushes in or out of the barn aisle.

2. Squeeze your horse out of the barn, ask him to turn, face, and wait. Give him a "long" break outside.

3. Squeeze him back in the barn, ask him to turn, face, and wait a moment, then send him back out.

4. Your goal is to create more draw to the outside of the barn by giving rest/scratches/food to him outside the barn. Continue this pattern until he would rather stay outside, then allow him to graze or have a big break outside the barn.

Savvy Tips
• The turn, face, and wait is one of the most important things in Squeeze Game. Be sure your horse is finding a standstill with his Zone 1 pointed at you, while you stand in neutral.

Troubleshooting
• *My horse wants to leave the barn and it's hard to send him back in.*
Great! You've achieved the goal of this exercise! Move on to another exercise where he can move his feet more, perhaps Circling or Sideways.
• *My horse gets panicked when outside the barn.*
This means that leaving the barn was too big of a step. As a reminder you can refer back to the "Comfort Zone" diagram at the beginning of the book. You need to go back to playing in the aisle with a focus on giving your horse rest when he is thinking away from the stalls/herd. You are trying to create a situation where it is your horse's idea to leave the barn, and he would rather be with you away from the herd/stalls.

33. Sideways Out Of Barn

Prerequisites
• Level 1 Sideways skills.

Outcomes
• Create a more responsive Sideways. As a result you will get Phase 2-3 responses.
• Get your horse more focused on you.
• Create 'draw' for your horse to leave the barn by building the rest on the outside of the barn.

Steps

1. Your horse is confident leaving the barn and it is time to make this more meaningful. As you drive your horse Sideways, pick a focus. If you are able to go Sideways without a fence then pick a focus off in the distance. If you need a fence to keep him from going forward, then use the outside of the barn.

2. Drive him Sideways to the point you picked away from his stall/barn door, and allow him to rest.

3. Keep picking new points around the barn "yard." You can start to pick points that take you right past the barn door and keep Driving until you get to your point, away from the door.
4. Keep this pattern going until you feel your horse becoming lighter and more willing to float Sideways away from the barn, then give him a big reward for his connection.

Savvy Tips

• Play Sideways on both sides of your horse. This is a perfect time to begin noticing which way is easier for your horse to go Sideways. You can start to help him gain strength and coordination on the tougher side by asking him to do it more often and by expecting increasing quality.
• As you and your horse increase your skills, you can ask for Sideways at trot and even at canter.

Troubleshooting

• *I feel awkward using the stick with my left hand, can I just keep it in my right hand?*
For your horse's sake, it is best to switch hands with the stick when you switch sides of your horse. To get more comfortable with the stick in your non-dominant hand, start carrying it with you everywhere you go in your non-dominant hand. The best way to get more comfortable with it is to use it. As you walk, pick different targets and see if you can aim and hit them with the string as you go past.

34. Spiral To The Grass

Prerequisites
- Level 1 and 2 Circling Game skills.
- A safe place to circle your horse outside of the barn/stall.

Outcomes
- Building 'draw' for your horse away from his buddy/barn.
- Causing you and your idea to become more comfortable. In this case, your idea is to take him to grass to eat.
- To have a confident horse eating grass away from his barn/buddy.

Steps

1. Once your horse is comfortable coming out of the barn and actually looking forward to coming out, you can start to play with more motion in bigger areas. After bringing your horse outside the barn, ask him to circle.

2. Once he is maintaining gait at walk or trot, pick a focus and begin to 'mosey' there. You will need to take your time as you go, allowing him to circle you as you move.
3. When he stops or turns to face you, pause your feet, then

send him. Once he is maintaining gait, you can begin to mosey again.

4. When you get to your point, offer your horse something he LOVES like treats, scratches, molasses water, rest, etc. Allow him to rest a long time here, then go back to the barn and repeat with a new, or farther away point.

Savvy Tips

• Keep a strong focus as you walk, and walk SLOWLY! If you move your feet faster than your horse, you will end up beating him to your point while you drag him along. Think about going with a mosey or "window shopping" speed.

• Begin by picking resting points that are fairly close to your barn so that your horse doesn't get worried or emotional while you are trying to allow him to rest.

Troubleshooting

• *My horse gets fast on the circle and is getting scared.*

Your horse may be getting emotional and releasing adrenaline. Try using a pattern to help him calm down – Figure 8 is a great pattern to use. You can also try soft changes of direction at walk, or transitions before he gets too "lost" to help him stay connected. These are great patterns because you can incorporate them into the exercise without getting off track from your focus.

*"Horses and humans
have mutual responsibilities."*

35. Driving From Zone 3 On A "Trail Ride"

Prerequisites
- Level 1+ Driving Game skills.
- Previous Driving exercises in stall and throughout the barn aisle. Your horse needs to be confident with these before he will be ready to play Driving Game farther away from his safety (comfort zone).

Outcomes
- Build confidence in new areas with your horse while you are in Zone 3 (the same zone you will be in when riding).
- Create a horse that is more self-confident in new environments and checks in with you for leadership and guidance.

Steps

1. After your horse is confident with you Driving from Zone 3 around his stall and the barn aisle, you are both ready to start going farther. Now pick a focus outside the barn and head there.

126

2. Once you get to the focus (away from the herd/barn/ stall) take a long rest.
3. Pick a focus inside the barn and when you get there immediately pick a new focus. When you arrive give rest/ feed/scratch.
4. Continue this pattern, building to farther and farther distances away from your horse's herd. Drive around the barn, to the paddock, etc. Each time you head back to the barn don't stop and each time you head away from the barn, take a long and meaningful rest.

Savvy Tips
• Pick distances away from the herd that offer your horse the opportunity to get in the learning zone without pushing him into the panic zone.
• Practice Driving from both sides, this is excellent preparation for riding and will serve you if you can smoothly and confidently direct your horse from either side.

Troubleshooting
• *My horse gets scared when I leave the barn.*
This may mean he has gone too close to the panic zone. Go back to where he is calm and confident, even if it is all the way back to his stall. Pick a new focus that isn't as far away as your last point. See if he can rest and relax here, if not, pick a focus that's even closer to where he was comfortable. Keep in mind we are trying to help him stretch his comfort and learning zones and not push him into the panic zone.

"Don't look where your horse is going, that's his job."

127

Well Done Completing This Section!

You have taken huge steps in improving your relationship with your horse and building a partnership your horse is glad to be a part of!

As A Reminder Of Where To Go From Here

Now that you have completed the exercises in this section you may find it useful to use additional sections and adjust the exercises to fit your situation. These sections will review some of the information you just covered and they will give you additional tools and perspectives for continuing to build your relationship.

Another option is to take what you have learned from this section and go straight to the exercises in the Riding section, keeping track of your program on the Partner Progress Pages.

Last, read over the Emergency Strategy section so that you will be better prepared for unforeseen situations if they arise.

At any time you feel you need a little "refresher" have quick read back over the theory section as a reminder to look at things from your horse's perspective.

SECTION 3

Horses Kept In
Pairs Or
With A Buddy

This section is focused on strategies for building
confidence in your horse when separating them from
the herd. These techniques will be most relevant
for horses that are kept with one other horse.
Once your horse is confident outside of the pen,
all exercises from "Horses Kept In The Herd" can be
used with 'the buddy' in place of 'the herd.'

Horsenality Filter: Horses Kept In Pairs

As you progress through the following section you may find the Horsenality filter below useful to help tailor each exercise to fit your individual horse.

LB Extrovert

- Keep having fun, play is this horse's middle name.
- Encourage his ideas by shaping them into yours.
- Specific exercises that will help this horse connect are: 36-40, 42-44, 46-50.

RB Extrovert

- Be aware of your horse's confidence bubble away from the herd and slowly build the distance.
- Keep things simple and easy to figure out.
- Keep your focus.
- Specific exercises that will help this horse connect are: 36-40, 42-50.

LB Introvert

- Show your horse that there is something in it for him.
- Start slow and specific, end with exuberance.
- Variety is important.
- Don't do the same thing more than 3 times without adding variety, or he will get bored.
- Specific exercises that will help this horse connect are: 36-44, 46, 48-50.

RB Introvert

- Remember you are "weaning" this horse from his herd.
- Waiting at the right time will build trust and confidence.
- Remember to use lots of approach and retreat, then re-approach.
- Specific exercises that will help this horse connect are: 36-46, 48-50.

Safety Reminders

Be aware of the other horse – in this situation you are building comfort and learning zones for two horses at the same time. The horse you have with you is developing self-confidence and confidence in you, whereas the horse left in the paddock has to rely on self-confidence alone.

Setting yourself up for success with just two horses can take some additional savvy. As you play with your horse you also need to stay aware of the other horse and their needs. This can be a particular challenge if your other horse wants to "get in your pocket" the whole time you are playing. If this is the case, rather than just keeping the other horse loose, there are some other options you might play with to cause your play session to be more enjoyable.

If the other horse ties, you may find a safe place to tie them and proceed with the exercises nearby, as if the horse was loose. Another option is to put them in a pen and play the same way. If you don't have a pen, you can set up a temporary one out of panels (you might even build this in the middle of the paddock). Another option is to feed the other horse some hay – anything to keep them occupied so you can focus on the horse you have a rope on. One other option is to have a Parelli buddy be a leader for the other horse and do the same exercises at the same time.

Catching Game Tips For A Herd Of Two

You can play the classic Parelli Catching Game. Also, remember Pat Parelli's suggestion of catching the easiest horse first. This may mean you have to adjust your play session slightly, but keep in mind that our goal is to build a relationship with your horse and create confidence in you as the leader. For this reason, sneaking up or cornering your horse is not a great way to start the relationship!

Examples Of Rewards Away From The Buddy

Rest, scratches, food, water/molasses water, grass, rolling.

Distance Away From Buddy For
Reward Progression

12 feet, 15 feet, 22 feet, 32 feet, 45 feet, other side of the paddock, rest outside paddock (be aware the next "big" step will come when you rest out of sight of the other horse), rest in the barn, rest in the arena, rest in the trailer, rest on the other side of the barn.

Level Recommendations

Adjust the exercise to fit your savvy level: Level 1 – 12-foot line, Level 2 – 22-foot line, Level 3-4 – 45-foot line.

Helpful References

Parelli Zones Of The Horse for reference as you read through the following section.

Seven Games Summary And Reminders

Principle Games

1. Friendly Game: This game is the Confidence Game – to help your horse gain confidence in people, places, changes and things. While playing this game you will use:

   • *Approach and Retreat*   • *Rhythm.*

2. Porcupine Game: This game is focused around the concept of teaching your horse to *Follow a Feel.*

3. Driving Game: This game is about getting your horse to *Follow a Suggestion.*

Purpose Games

4. Yo-Yo Game: The to and fro game. By using this game you help your horse balance *Backwards and Forwards.*

5. Circling Game: The purpose of circling to help your horse learn his *Responsibilities.*

6. Sideways Game: This game is all about *Lateral Movements.*

7. Squeeze Game: Also known as the *Matador Game.* This game is about *Shortening Your Horse's Flight Line* and helping them build confidence in situations they perceive as a Squeeze or as claustrophobic.

36. Friendly Game In Motion

Prerequisites
- Level 1 ground skills knowledge.
- Ability to move the other horse or stay aware of their location and emotions, so you can stay safe.

Outcomes
- Creating confidence with rhythmic motion while your horse's feet are in motion.
- Having a horse that can read the difference between the Friendly Game and the Driving Game through your body language.

Steps
1. Warm your horse up with a little Friendly Game with the stick and string over their back.

2. While standing beside your horse, ask them to circle around you (close range Circling Game). Allow the Carrot Stick to rest on their back as they circle.
3. Now you are going to begin moving your stick and playing Friendly Game in motion. You can start this by just rubbing your horse with the Friendly motion. You are looking for them to maintain their rhythm as they circle.
4. As you build, you can play this same game and toss the rope over their back with increasing amounts of energy. As your horse relaxes into this exercise you can turn it

into Zone 3 Driving and drive your horse away from his buddy the appropriate distance.

Savvy Tips

- This can be a good exercise to use with two horses in the pasture, sometimes the Friendly motion of your stick can be enough to cause the other horse to stay far enough away that you can play safely.
- Keep the energy in your body Friendly as your horse circles you. This will help your horse read the situation and realize they don't need to move faster or away from you.

Troubleshooting

- *My horse gets worried and runs around me when I start to move my stick.*

  You can go back to Friendly Game at the standstill to help re-establish confidence with Friendly Game. After your horse is able to accept Friendly Game at the standstill, ask them for close range Circling Game again. Check in and be sure they are confident with the Carrot Stick resting on their back; if not, use your strategies for releasing for relaxation in Friendly Game. If they are confident, then begin by slowly moving the stick, like you're giving them a massage – be sure your energy is Friendly and slowly increase the intensity from there. If they get scared again, play approach and retreat until they get a little better.

"Your horse doesn't care how much you know,
until he's knows how much you care."

37. Extreme Friendly Game By Buddy

Prerequisites
- Level 1 ground skills knowledge.
- Ability to move the other horse or stay aware of their location, so you can stay safe.

Outcomes
- Creating confidence with extreme rhythmic motion.
- Creating a situation where your horse develops more draw to leave his buddy by receiving more rest and relaxation away from his buddy.

Steps

1. Now that your horse is confident with regular Friendly Game, and maybe even Friendly Game in motion, we can add ENERGY! First, be sure that even when you get your energy up you are not becoming emotional or intimidating (think about looking like a happy Labrador Retriever).
2. Using your stick and string, play an energetic Friendly Game, stretching your horse's confidence. He'll know the stick/string is Friendly because of the energy in your body.

3. Begin to expand by moving to different zones. Keep your rope at an appropriate length in case your horse gets

136

worried. You can use your rope to "lift to stop the drift."

4. You can try different distances away from your horse. As he gains confidence and relaxes, offer him a feel and lead him away from his buddy to a patch of grass (whatever distance away that is appropriate for him at this stage).

Savvy Tips

- If your horse has not played this game before or seems to get worried, remember to play approach and retreat. You can use distance to play approach and retreat by moving closer and farther away, or you can use energy to play approach and retreat by using less energy and then more energy to help your horse gain confidence.
- As you move to other zones be sure you are safe, do not put yourself in a position where you could get kicked.

Troubleshooting

- *My horse is scared of the stick, I can't even touch him with it.*

  He needs to develop confidence with the Carrot Stick as an extension of you. If your horse is worried with you even holding the stick, you will still need to play approach and retreat. You may need to start by not facing your horse: With the Carrot Stick in your hand, turn your belly button away from your horse and walk away, with him following you. Move the Carrot Stick around in front of you until he is confident, then turn around and walk the same direction but backwards while continuing to move your stick. Do not try to touch your horse, just allow him to follow and gain confidence. As this progresses you can slow your feet, hold still, then advance to touching him. Before he gets worried, retreat away again to help him gain confidence.

38. Clipping By Buddy

Prerequisites
- Level 1 Friendly Game savvy.
- Clippers or a massager that makes clipper buzzing noises.

Outcomes
- Helping your horse become more confident with the clippers.
- Creating a situation where your horse develops more draw to leave his buddy by receiving more rest and relaxation away from his buddy, by using the clippers near his buddy.

Steps

1. Take your battery clippers or massager (the handheld massagers make great tools for helping prepare horses for real clippers) with you to your horse. Begin by playing Friendly Game with the tool turned off.

2. Progress to having the clippers on and clipping his legs (you can choose to clip them or just pretend as a preparation exercise).

3. Proceed to clipping the ears and chin (again only actually clip your horse if it is appropriate for you).
4. Finish your clipping job and take your horse the appropriate distance away from his buddy to allow him to rest.

Savvy Tips

- To keep yourself safe, be sure your horse is confident and that you don't compromise your safety. Keep your rope in hand while clipping and set yourself up for success by making a program of Friendly Game with the massager/ clipper simulator before you try the clippers.
- If your horse is dirty and you don't want to dull your clippers, you can use a hand massager to simulate the same exercise, or you can use your clippers and rub them in the same place you would clip without actually clipping.

Troubleshooting

- *My horse is avoiding the clippers.*
  Use more Friendly Game with approach and retreat. Give your horse the time he needs to get confident; remember, "Take the time it takes now, so it takes less time next time."

*"Put your heart in your hand
and rub your horse with your heart."*

39. Vet Prep By Buddy

Prerequisites
• Level 1 savvy with ground skills.

Outcomes
• Helping your horse become more confident with behaviors and tools your vet may use.
• Creating a situation where your horse develops more draw to leave his buddy by receiving more rest and relaxation away from his buddy.

Steps

1. The biggest thing we can help our horses with for veterinarians is needle prep. You can use a toothpick to simulate a needle.

2. While standing beside your horse, with your rope still in hand, rub your horse on the neck where the vet would pull a coggins; you can even tap him on the neck. Continue this until your horse relaxes, then stop.

3. Repeat, then finish with a pinch or toothpick poke, keeping the pressure until your horse relaxes his neck.

4. Repeat this process until your horse is relaxed and understands that in order to stop the pressure from your "needle" he needs to soften and relax. Now, bring him away from his buddy and allow him to rest.

Savvy Tips

- As you are preparing your horse, think of how other people sometimes approach horses – make sure you also prepare your horse for fast and abrupt approaches. This is a big piece in helping your horse to be prepared for vets/farriers/etc.
- If you don't have a toothpick you could also just pinch the skin.
- You can use Porcupine Game on the halter to help lower your horse's head so they can find relaxation.

Troubleshooting

- *My horse is really worried about needles.*
  Take your time. You may need to make a program (7+ days) of just rubbing and tapping until you get relaxation, then proceeding, taking your time with each step along the way.

*"Horses know what happens,
before what happens, happens."*

40. Farrier Prep By Buddy

Prerequisites
• Level 1-2 savvy with ground skills.

Outcomes
• Helping your horse become more confident with behaviors and tools your farrier may use.
• Creating a situation where your horse develops more draw to leave his buddy by receiving more rest and relaxation away from his buddy.

Steps

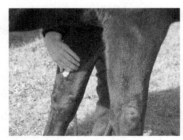

1. While your horse is hanging out by his buddy start by asking your horse to pick up his front feet by squeezing the chestnut.

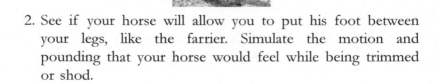

2. See if your horse will allow you to put his foot between your legs, like the farrier. Simulate the motion and pounding that your horse would feel while being trimmed or shod.

3. Now, go to your horse's back feet and ask him to offer you the foot by squeezing the cap of the hock. Again, see if you can cradle the hoof on your legs and simulate the motion of the farrier.

4. Repeat this process until your horse is willing and cooperative. Then when you are ready to allow him to rest, take him the appropriate distance away from his buddy and give him a reward.

Savvy Tips

- As you are thinking of truly preparing your horse for the farrier, also simulate the energy that he approaches your horse with. You can help your horse get ready by approaching him with this same energy.

- As you are preparing, keep in mind that sometimes it takes the farrier an hour to do a horse's hooves. Be sure you are helping prepare your horse to have the patience to help the farrier get his job done to the best of his ability.

Troubleshooting

- *My horse keeps pulling his hoof away.*
  Keep in mind the release is what teaches. So, if he pulls away and then gets to rest he will learn that pulling away gets a reward. On the flip side, you don't want to punish him for pulling away. Simply, don't give him a rest, pick the foot back up and try to time your release for the moment he is willing. Also, if he keeps taking his foot away he may need you to move his feet more, using a productive pattern (Figure 8, etc.) before he is ready to keep his feet still.

Ways To Advance This Exercise

- One way to advance the quality of your horse standing for the farrier can be by creating a game out of it. You might play some games that require more movement and then make the hoof cradle the resting point, so that your horse almost starts to offer putting their foot in the position the farrier needs it to be.

41. Lead By Leg

Prerequisites
• Level 2 rope handling skills and knowledge of the Porcupine Game.

Outcomes
• Teaching your horse to follow a feeling from the rope around his leg, responding at Phase 2-3 with understanding.
• Cause your horse to find relaxation while he is farther away from his buddy, by giving him rest away from his buddy when he follows a feel.

Steps

1. With your 12-foot line attached to the halter, use your 22-foot rope around your horse's leg to play Friendly Game until they are confident.

2. Holding both ends of the 22-foot line, begin playing Porcupine Game and asking your horse to move his leg from the pressure. Release as soon as he yields.
3. Continue playing this with his front leg until he accepts

144

you moving his leg in all different positions and is able to follow the feeling.

4. As he becomes more willing, see if you can ask him to yield away from his buddy and allow him to rest away from his buddy.

Savvy Tips

- After your horse becomes willing on his front legs you can advance to his hind legs.
- As you play be sure your horse is following the feel on the rope and not just following you. This game is about following the feel on his leg and learning to yield to it.
- Keep in mind the Phases of Porcupine Game:
  1. Hair, 2. Skin, 3. Muscle, 4. Bone.

Troubleshooting

- *My horse will not move his leg!*
  While continuing the pressure of Porcupine Game, begin to tap your horse's coronet band with the toe of your boot. Using rhythmic pressure to support Porcupine can be an effective way to add motivation for your horse to yield and become more responsive.
- *My horse gets worried when I put the rope around his leg.*
  He may need you to play more approach and retreat with Friendly Game, using the rope to build his confidence, before you begin to ask for Porcupine. If the rope is too much, you can also use your Carrot Stick to practice approaching and retreating with rubbing.

Ways To Advance This Exercise

- As your horse gets good at this game you can have a lot of fun with advancing the games you play while the rope is on your horse's leg. This can eventually lead to circles with nothing on your horse but the rope on the leg.

42. Backwards Circles

Prerequisites
• Level 3 ground skills and development with your horse.

Outcomes
• Building your horse's 'maintain gait' responsibility by adding backwards.
• Creating a situation where your horse can be near his buddy and can move his feet. When he begins to focus on you he gets the opportunity to rest with you and away from his buddy.

Steps
1. For this exercise we will use the same principles as we do in Circling Game, mainly; maintain gait. For this exercise, you will ask your horse to circle around you backwards. Start by standing in Zone 3 holding your Carrot Stick and string.
2. Ask your horse to back 2-3 steps. You can use your Carrot Stick for support if he doesn't respond to your energy and rope wiggling.

3. Drive your horse's FQ over a step or two (this will help keep your horse lined up to make a circle around you). Now ask for backwards again, then repeat the process.
4. Be sure to reward him each time he puts in a good effort.

Also, just like Circling Game, each time he responds bring your body to neutral and give him the opportunity to maintain gait backwards. As soon as he offers one step of maintaining gait, give him a big reward.

Savvy Tips

- To teach your horse to maintain a circle around you backwards you can use the corner of the pasture to help "hold" your horse on the shape.
- By using Driving Game on the FQ and Driving Zone 1 away, you will in effect keep the HQ aimed in a circle around you. In the beginning, this circle may look a little "sloppy" but that is okay, just go with your horse and help them learn the pattern.
- As you are teaching your horse to maintain gait backwards, remember to reward for the slightest try. Even if he backs with a little more lightness, this is a reason to reward. When you want to ask him for backwards again, remember to start at Phase 1 and give him the opportunity to respond, even if you think it will take Phase 3-4 to get a result.

Troubleshooting

- *My horse is backing straight and I can't get him to think about a circle.*

You may need to play the game by moving your feet to stay in Zone 3 for a while. You will do this by playing as you would if you were Driving from Zone 3. Keep your feet moving with your horse and practice 2 steps back, 2 steps over with the FQ. When your horse begins to understand the game, you will be able to move your feet less and less, and eventually be able to keep them in your circle.

43. Strengthening Your "Yo"

Prerequisites
- Level 1 ground skills knowledge.
- Ability to move the other horse or stay aware of their location, so you can stay safe.

Outcomes
- Creating draw towards you and increasing the lightness of your draw, by using the buddy to your advantage.
- Taking your horse's idea of coming to his buddy and using it to get him more focused on you and increase your draw.
- Allowing your horse to rest with you and away from his buddy.

Steps

1. Drive or Yo-Yo your horse backwards away from his buddy, give him about 7 seconds rest.

2. Draw him to you by combing the rope steadily stronger and stronger until he draws to you. Once he is with you, give him a big break (treats, rest, scratches, hang out time).

3. Repeat this process until he backs with lightness and comes to you with lightness (at least 1% better than where you started).
4. When you get closer to the lightness and responsiveness you were aiming for, draw him to you and allow him to rest with you, away from his buddy.

Savvy Tips

- This is a great exercise to help improve your draw because you will be using the draw to your horse's buddy, as well as the draw to you.
- If your horse's draw is very strong but he isn't as good at backing, you can reverse this exercise to balance him out. You stand away from the buddy, back him towards his buddy and then draw him to you.

Troubleshooting

- *My horse is leaning on the rope and won't draw back to me.*
  You can use Driving Game to support your Friendly Game. When your horse is leaning on the rope, begin rhythm with the Carrot Stick until your horse comes off of the rope. Your Carrot Stick can tap the air or you can use it to tap the rope, the goal is that you are setting your horse up to be less comfortable to lean on the rope.

"Pressure motivates, but release teaches."

44. Backwards Weave

Prerequisites
• Level 1 ground skills knowledge.
• Ability to move the other horse or stay aware of their location, so that you can stay safe.

Outcomes
• The communication to steer your horse while going backwards, by being able to complete the pattern.
• Increasing your horse's responsiveness while going backwards, by getting Phase 2-3 responses.
• Allowing your horse to rest at the end of the exercise away from his buddy.

Steps
1. You will need to have a weave set up. You can use cones, or markers, or just a specific space in the grass; you just need to know where your mark is so that you can be particular and consistent.

2. Drive your horse backwards while you are in Zone 1, keep a focus on where you want him to go.

3. To help him make the turn around the cones, use your HQ yields to influence his HQ – it's like steering a wheelbarrow.

4. When you get to the last cone, back a half circle around to bring your horse back to the weave pattern. Keep going like this until your horse is backing with responsiveness, then back them away from their buddy for a big reward.

Savvy Tips

- Remember, the better your horse goes backwards and sideways, the better he does everything else. Also, sometimes you can help your horse learn how to back straight by backing him on arcs – the weave is a great pattern for this.
- You can also play this game by using Porcupine Game, either on the halter or on your horse's nose.
- Be sure to give your horse little releases as you play so that he doesn't lose incentive to keep backing. Also, make sure you are going back to Phase 1 after he responds, so that you don't get stuck 'nagging' him at Phase 3.

Troubleshooting

- *My horse seems to get worried about backing close to the cone/barrel.* In the end, winning the Friendly Game with these obstacles will be the answer. You can play some Squeeze Game to help him with this, or you can continue playing the weave and just back a bigger arc around the cones/barrels so that he doesn't feel such a tight Squeeze.

45. Backwards 'S'

Prerequisites
• Level 2+ ground and rope handling skills with your horse.
• Consistent footing so that you are safe to walk backwards.

Outcomes
• Creating confidence in your horse to switch eyes with you in Zone 1.
• Building draw towards you and away from his buddy by giving him rest when he is focused on you.

Steps
1. Start in front of your horse, with open space behind you. Begin by softly sending your horse out and around you.

2. As soon as your horse starts moving, begin slowly walking your feet backwards in a straight line. Before he gets to your shoulder, use your rope to direct him back in the other direction.

3. Keep your feet moving steadily backwards and allow your horse to get almost to your shoulder, then redirect him with your rope (and stick if needed for the new direction).

4. Continue this pattern with your horse making an 'S' or serpentine towards you, until your horse is really putting effort into drawing towards you. Allow the pattern to end away from his buddy and give him a big reward.

Savvy Tips

- This exercise is great at building draw and confidence in your horse. If however, he is a little pushy you may go forward to the next exercise "Falling Leaf" to help balance out your drive and draw with some extra Driving Game.
- Backwards 'S' can be a good tool to help your change of direction on the circle.
- Making a straight line with your feet will help during this exercise. You can do this by picking a far off focus and using your peripheral vision to help you spot when to redirect your horse.
- This exercise is more about softly redirecting Zone 1 rather than Driving. If possible, use just the rope to redirect and then if needed you can support with your Carrot Stick.

Troubleshooting

- *My horse is coming too close and I can't get him to send away.*
  This means you are experiencing a strong draw, and also that it's time to balance this draw with the Driving Game. The next exercise, falling leaf, should help balance the drive and help you get some personal space back.

46. Falling Leaf

Prerequisites
• Level 2 ground skills and rope handling.

Outcomes
• Balancing 'draw' with 'drive' by getting light (Phase 2-3) responses to the HQ and FQ yields.
• Developing equal responses on the right and left.
• Creating draw away from your horse's buddy by offering rest and rewards when he gets farther away from his buddy.

Steps
1. Start by sending your horse out on a circle. You need to have a focus picked out up ahead and in the distance.
2. At the same time your horse moves off on the circle, begin moving your feet forward. Right before your horse passes your shoulder, ask him to disengage and drive the FQ around to the new direction.

3. Keep your feet drifting forwards, and before your horse passes your other shoulder, disengage the HQ and send the FQ the new direction.

4. Continue playing this falling leaf pattern with your horse going from 9 o'clock to 3 o'clock. When he is responsive and you have worked your way away from his buddy, give him a big reward.

Savvy Tips
- This is a great exercise to counterbalance the Backwards 'S' exercise and you can use these two exercises in the same session to assess your drive and draw.
- A straight line will help you and your horse during this exercise. Keep a far off focus and allow your peripheral vision to help you.
- Be sure you are Driving the HQ and getting two eyes before Driving the FQ.
- If you miss getting your horse to turn before passing your shoulder, just try again on the next lap. That's the handy thing about circles, your horse will be in the same position again, soon.

Troubleshooting
- *My horse is not disengaging.*
  As you continue to ask, reach down your rope, take an arm length out, and ask again. Repeat this process until he tries to disengage. By shortening the rope you are making it harder for him to run around you in a circle and to ignore what you are asking.

Ways To Advance This Exercise
- This can be a fun way to set your horse up for playing a game of cutting with you at Liberty. Where you pretend to be a cow and your horse makes moves like a cutting horse to not allow you to get by. As you play towards this, keep in mind if your horse is heavy on the rope he would most likely be leaving you if you were at Liberty.

47. Figure 8 By Buddy

Prerequisites
- Level 1 ground skills knowledge.
- Ability to move the other horse or stay aware of their location, so you can stay safe.

Outcomes
- By causing your horse to move his feet near his buddy and allowing him to rest away from his buddy, you will create more confidence away from his buddy.
- To give your horse an opportunity to move his feet until he is ready to stop and come rest with you.
- Developing positive patterns that can build to flying lead changes.

Steps

1. Set up a figure 8 pattern with cones, barrels, poop, or anything to give you and your horse a 'marker.' You will also need a marker for your feet so that you don't drift too far and you know where your goal is. Start by sending your horse out on the pattern.

2. As he begins to follow your focus, be sure you come back to neutral in between requests so you are not 'nagging' him.
3. Continue the figure 8 pattern until he is taking the responsibility to maintain it and you are able to get your feet closer to holding still.
4. When he is responsive and focused on you, take him away from his buddy and allow him to rest.

Savvy Tips
• Setting this pattern up as a responsibility can make a huge change for your horse. By doing this you are causing him to use his brain and you get to do less!
• If your horse gets easily bored, you can alternate between Circling Game and figure 8. This way it helps you get some impulsion back and helps your horse stay connected with you and your body language.

Troubleshooting
• *My horse is getting "stuck" behind the cone/barrel and won't keep going on the pattern.*
This is a common puzzle horses give us in this pattern. Remember that it is the horse's responsibility to maintain gait and then direction. First, address the maintain gait "issue" even if it means he comes off the pattern. Then, once you have maintain gait established you can ask him to stay on the pattern.

48. Rock Slide

Prerequisites
• Level 2 ground skills.

Outcomes
• Build a balanced Sideways where your horse easily yields his HQ and stops drifting forwards.
• Create draw away from his buddy by providing rest and relaxation when he gets there.
• Improving backwards and sideways in your horse.

Steps

1. Begin by picking a focus and lining your horse up so that he will back towards your focus, with you in Zone 1.
2. After backing him for 5-7 steps, drive Zone 1 until you are lined up in Zone 3, then drive your horse Sideways still heading towards your focus.

3. After 5-7 steps, drive your horse's HQ until he is backing again, still going towards your focus.

4. After 5-6 steps of backing, drive the FQ in the other direction. Once you are lined up in Zone 3, drive your horse Sideways. You can repeat this as many times as needed. When you are ready to stop, finish with backwards and allow your horse to rest away from his buddy.

Savvy Tips

- This is a great exercise to help horses get better at Sideways without a fence. Horses naturally want to go forwards and lag the HQ on Sideways, Rock Slide is a great exercise to balance this natural tendency. Also, by ending on backwards you are helping to emphasize this new pattern.
- Picking a strong focus and staying straight is important to the quality of this exercise.

Troubleshooting

- *My horse keeps walking forwards.*
  Think of the saying "Do less sooner, rather than more later." By having a strong focus you will be able to tell when your horse has shifted his weight a little forward and can correct him by wiggling the rope (Yo-Yo Phases, but in an up and down wiggle) until he yields backwards.

Ways To Advance This Exercise

- Rock Slide can build to being a great game to play with your horse on the way from the pasture back to the barn and from the saddling area to where you will be riding. Because you have a focus and are going somewhere while moving your horse's feet and checking out his yields, it can serve as part of your 'pre-flight checks.' (You can find out more about pre-flight checks in the Parelli program).

49. Jumps By Buddy

Prerequisites
• Level 1 ground skills.

Outcomes
• Create a more confident and athletic partner by playing Squeeze Game, maintaining rhythm through the Squeeze, and turning and facing easily on the other side.
• Set up a pattern where your horse moves his feet when he is with his buddy and finds rest and relaxation when he is away from his buddy.

Steps

1. Set your horse up to play Squeeze Game by his buddy. You can use jumps, ditches, logs, poop, barrels, anything that you can think of for a Squeeze. After squeezing him over or through the obstacle, cause him to turn, face, and wait for 7 seconds.

2. Pick a new obstacle and send him to it, Squeeze, turn, face, wait.
3. Pick a new obstacle and repeat the process, each time you

are giving him a little reward for the Squeeze. You might even set up a pattern of Squeezes around his buddy in a circle.

4. When he seems focused on you and looks like he might be ready for a break, Squeeze him away from his buddy and give him a big reward at the appropriate distance from his buddy.

Savvy Tips
- Remember your stages of Squeeze game:
  1. Send.
  2. Allow (this is an important Phase and will keep you from 'nagging' your horse while he is "doing the job").
  3. Turn, face, and wait.
- If your horse is having trouble saying "yes" to the Squeeze, you might try asking while he is going towards his buddy, versus away from his buddy. This small shift can be enough for horses to make a change.
- You can combine this game with Circles and Sideways, etc., by your horse's buddy, then give a big rest away to help emphasize comfort away from the buddy.

Troubleshooting
- *My horse won't do any of the Squeezes that I ask of him.*
  You may need to ask him for a smaller "puzzle" until he has a pattern of "yes" responses. If he won't go over a jump, see if you can find a smaller one to build a good pattern. If he won't Squeeze between you and the fence, back up 3 steps and try again. If he still won't go, back up 3 more steps. This will create a bigger "door" for him to go through and will take off some of the pressure of the Squeeze.

50. Trailer Load By Buddy

Prerequisites
• Level 1 ground skills.

Outcomes
• Create a more confident and athletic partner by playing with the trailer near your buddy.
• Increasing your horse's confidence to stay in the trailer, where he offers to stay in even with the door open.
• Set up a pattern where your horse moves his feet when he is with his buddy and finds rest and relaxation when he is away from his buddy (in the trailer).

Steps
1. This exercise is an extension of Squeeze Game, and is a great thing to play if you have a trailer available near your horse's buddy. If your horse doesn't like loading, one little thing you can do to help is set the trailer up so that the nose of the trailer is pointing towards your horse's buddy.
2. After preparing your horse for trailer loading and playing some "Touch It" games, ask your horse to load.

3. If he doesn't go all the way in or comes right back out, you can play some Sideways and/or Falling Leaf and Rock Slide around the trailer and his buddy.
4. Head back to the trailer and offer it to him as an opportunity to rest, again. You may need to repeat this process

several times, but keep in mind that you are trying to build his confidence away from his buddy, we are just using the trailer as a tool to build this confidence.

Savvy Tips

- This is an extension of Squeeze Game, so if your horse is having trouble with the trailer you can pause aiming for the trailer and in the meantime expand your Squeeze Game as much as possible. Get him confident going onto things, under things, through things, and combinations thereof. These are all pieces of the trailering Squeeze and will help your horse get more confident about the trailer without having to go there, yet.
- Remember the first two stages of Squeeze Game as they still apply in trailer loading: 1. Send. 2. ALLOW (be careful that you don't get caught asking a trying horse to try, it's important that your body language is 'allowing' and not 'begging' him to go in the trailer/Squeeze).

Troubleshooting

- *My horse doesn't care about the trailer and going in but he won't stay in.*

At this stage that is okay, just count how many seconds he stays in and that will give you a starting point. When he comes out, simply ask him to move his feet by playing some of the games or patterns. When he seems ready for a break, offer him the option of the trailer. If he comes right back out again, repeat the process. When he stays for 3-4+ seconds longer than the first time, quit for the day and make a program of the trailer game.

Well Done Completing This Section!

You have taken huge steps in improving your relationship with your horse and building a partnership your horse is glad to be a part of!

As A Reminder Of Where To Go From Here

Now that you have completed the exercises in this section, you may find it useful to use additional sections and adjust the exercises to fit your situation. These sections will review some of the information you just covered and they will give you additional tools and perspectives for continuing to build your relationship.

Another option is to take what you have learned from this section and go straight to the exercises in the Riding section, keeping track of your program on the Partner Progress Pages.

Last, read over the Emergency Strategy section so that you will be better prepared for unforeseen situations if they arise.

At any time you feel you need a little "refresher," have a quick read back over the theory section as a reminder to look at things from your horse's perspective.

SECTION 4

Riding
With A Buddy
Horse(s)

This section is focused on strategies
for building confidence in your horse when
separating them from the herd.
These techniques will be most relevant
for horses that are being ridden together
and are drawn to one another.

Horsenality Filter: Riding With A Buddy Horse

As you progress through the following section you may find the Horsenality filter below useful to help tailor each exercise to fit your individual horse.

LB Extrovert

- Allowing this horse movement is key.
- Variety within your training will help him stay willing.
- If it gets too athletic – get off, this horse needs to move his feet to become mentally focused.

RB Extrovert

- Directing this horse's movement onto positive patterns is important.
- Use patterns to create relaxation and confidence.
- If he gets too athletic – get off, this horse needs to move his feet to become mentally focused.

LB Introvert

- Variety!
- Start slow to get him mentally engaged, allow him to offer the energy.
- Do not allow this horse to talk you into "pushing" every stride to keep them going – they can feel a fly.

RB Introvert

- Patterns and not pushing this horse while he's emotional or in the panic zone are important keys.
- Start slow, wait for the confidence to come and then they will offer more.
- Be sure not to force this horse at Phase 1 and 2.

Safety Reminders

Be aware of the other horse(s). In this situation you are building comfort and learning zones for at least two horses at the same time. In this situation you need to communicate effectively with the other rider(s). Before starting your ride, be sure you are both on the same page about the goal and priorities of your ride.

Rewards Away From The Buddy

Rest, scratches, food, water/molasses water, grass.

Distance Away From Buddy For Reward

12 feet, 15 feet, 22 feet, 32 feet, 45 feet, etc.

Level Recommendations

Adjust the exercise to fit your savvy level: Level 2 – walk, trot, get off if things get fast or unconfident; Level 3-4 – walk, trot, canter, be a good coach for yourself and get off when you need to.

Helpful References

Parelli Zones Of The Horse for reference as you read through the following section.

Seven Games Summary And Reminders

Principle Games

1. Friendly Game: This game is the Confidence Game – to help your horse gain confidence in people, places, changes and things. While playing this game you will use:

• *Approach and Retreat*   • *Rhythm.*

2. Porcupine Game: This game is focused around the concept of teaching your horse to *Follow a Feel.*

3. Driving Game: This game is about getting your horse to *Follow a Suggestion.*

Purpose Games

4. Yo-Yo Game: The to and fro game. By using this game you help your horse balance *Backwards and Forwards.*

5. Circling Game: The purpose of circling to help your horse learn his *Responsibilities.*

6. Sideways Game: This game is all about *Lateral Movements.*

7. Squeeze Game: Also known as the *Matador Game.* This game is about *Shortening Your Horse's Flight Line* and helping them build confidence in situations they perceive as a Squeeze or as claustrophobic.

51. Sideways Dance

Prerequisites
- Safety and communication while riding, Level 2 riding skills.
- A buddy rider and horse who are willing to work with you and adjust to help you with what your horse needs.

Outcomes
- Improve your Sideways by getting lighter responses, building to Sideways off of your intention.
- Having fun with some pair exercises while improving your Sideways.
- Increasing your horse's motivation to drift away from his buddy by moving his feet while he is near his buddy and allowing him to rest when he is away from his buddy.

Steps

1. As you are riding beside or in line with your buddy horse, ask your horse to yield Sideways away from his buddy. Start with only 2-3 steps, then allow him to rest (the rest may be you putting your hand in neutral while you continue walking or trotting by your buddy).

2. As he is resting he may drift back to his buddy, this is okay, just ask for Sideways away again (the same number of steps) and offer him rest away from his buddy, again.

3. You may have to repeat this 10-20 times before he thinks it's a good idea to stay a few feet away from his buddy. If he is willing to stay away in the beginning, then after your rest, ask him to walk back to his buddy and push him Sideways away again and allow him to rest away.
4. Continue increasing this distance until you are able to go 45 feet+ away with your horse staying calm, and increasing his draw to space away from his buddy.

Savvy Tips

• As you ask your horse for Sideways away, remember the technique of "lift to stop the drift." If your horse is going too forward use your reins to stop the forward motion.
• If you aren't yet able to ask for Sideways without the rail, you can do this on the rail. Just arrange your buddy next to the rail so that you can use the rail for Sideways.

Troubleshooting

- *My horse keeps going back to his buddy as soon as I try and get him to "rest."*

  This is to be expected, he is drawn to his buddy for safety at the moment. There are several things you can do. First, stick with it without getting mean or mad. Second, try to decrease the distance you are asking for him to go when traveling Sideways away – you may need to start by asking for just a step away.

- *My friend/buddy is getting bored.*

  If you feel ready, you can practice this same exercise in motion or down a trail, where your target and rest point become relative as you travel. Just keep a clear vision of the distance you are away from your buddy at the resting 'point.' This way your buddy can continue with their ride as usual and you can develop your horse's confidence away from his buddy.

*"If you're using your reins,
he's not using his brain."*

52. HQ/FQ Ballet

Prerequisites
- A willing horse and human buddy horse pair.
- Safety and communication while riding.

Outcomes
- Improve your HQ and FQ yields by adding some forwards after the maneuver.
- Achieving flow through the moves, and lightness (Phase 2-3) response.
- Increasing your horse's motivation to be comfortable away from his buddy by moving his feet while he is near his buddy and allowing him to rest when he is away from his buddy.

Steps
1. You can do this exercise while your buddy is holding still or while you are traveling around the arena/down the trail. While you are next to your buddy, begin by asking for indirect rein (move the HQ) until it is yielding softly.

2. Then use the same rein in a direct rein to ask the FQ to come around until you are pointing in the same direction as your buddy.
3. Continue this HQ yield followed by FQ yield like a ballet dancer until your horse becomes a little lighter/better at the exercise.

4. Allow him to rest away from the buddy. If you are walking down the trail/rail "rest" may be simply walking forward in a straight line, rather than doing HQ and FQ yields.

Savvy Tips

- Be aware of where your buddy is while you do this exercise, you do not want to set them up to get kicked while you are turning your horse.
- Remember the goal is to cause being with your horse's buddy to be more "work," and being away from his buddy to become easy. If you need a break or you need to think about what you were supposed to do, try to allow your horse to rest a little ways from his buddy so that he is not continuing a pattern of rest at his buddy.

Troubleshooting

- *My horse wants to kick his buddy.*
  First, be sure you are at a safe distance away so that his buddy will not get kicked. Second, if your horse is trying to kick, you will want to turn his nose towards your buddy, this will aim his kicking end away and help to keep your buddy safe.
- *I'm getting confused as to which rein and leg to use.*
  If you are turning to the right, you will ask your horse to move his HQ with your right rein in an indirect rein position, and your right leg. Then to finish the move you will use your right rein to lift up and out to open the door for the FQ to come through and your left leg to push the FQ over.

53. Soft Touch Comfort Zone Stretch

Prerequisites
- Level 3 riding skills.
- A willing buddy horse and rider.

Outcomes
- Improving your feel by practicing soft touch.
- Increasing your horse's motivation to be comfortable away from his buddy, by giving him something to focus on while he is near his buddy and allowing him to rest when he is away from his buddy.

Steps

1. As you are traveling forward with your horse, ask for soft touch while he continues to follow his buddy.
2. Hold this soft touch for as long or short as you like, but wait to release until your horse gives you a nice soft feeling. Pick the timing of your release so that you are away from your buddy when you release (this may start at just 4-5 feet away).

3. Now that you are away from your buddy, keep traveling in the same direction, but go back to a casual rein/FreeStyle rein position to allow your horse to have a rest.
4. Your horse may drift back to his buddy, this is okay, take the opportunity once he is there to practice your soft touch again. When you are ready to give him a break, increase the distance from your buddy then go back to FreeStyle.

Savvy Tips
- To pick up a soft touch, use the first 3 steps of the Parelli 9-Step Back up.
  1. Lift the reins with one hand.
  2. Slide your other hand down both reins, all the way to the neck.
  3. Separate the reins, one in each hand with your fingers pointing forward (not gripped around the reins).
- This can be a great little tool to use on the trail, just try not to use it to "hold your horse back." You want to increase the distance from your buddy more laterally to begin with. By increasing the distance from holding your horse back you are more likely to create a sling shot effect.

Troubleshooting
- *My horse pulls the reins out of my hands, continually!*
  He may need a more steady feel to help him find the release. Be sure you are on your balance point (so that he can't unseat you by pulling the reins), then ask for soft feel (go to step 7 of 9-Step Back up), this will allow you to close your hands on the reins and give a steadier feel, one that your horse can respect.

54. Beep-Beep

Prerequisites
- A willing buddy horse rider who has confidence using the stick while on their horse.
- Safety while riding your horse/Level 2 FreeStyle riding skills.

Outcomes
- Build a pattern where it is your horse's idea to stay away from the horse in front, while you focus on keeping him straight.
- Causing your horse to be uncomfortable when he is close to the buddy horse.
- Building motivation to stay away from his buddy by causing him to be more comfortable while he is away.

Steps
1. For this exercise you will need to be following your buddy horse and the buddy rider will need to have a Carrot Stick.

2. Your job while following your buddy is to keep your horse's nose pointed at the buddy horse's tail, and to let your buddy horse rider know when your horse is too close to their horse's tail.
3. They will begin by swinging the Carrot Stick over their horse's HQ towards your horse's Zone 1, then they will begin backing. Your job is to stay straight and allow the

backing horse in front of you and the Carrot Stick to back your horse.

4. Once your horse has backed away, carry on forward down the "trail" until your horse is too close, then repeat.

Savvy Tips
- The brilliance behind this exercise is that you get to be the "good guy!" Normally on trail rides we hold our horses back to keep them from the horse in front – this makes us seem like the bad guy, keeping our horses from what they want. However, by just keeping your horse straight he discovers it is a good idea to stay away from the Carrot Stick swinging randomly from the backing horse in front of him, and it becomes his idea to give that horse space.
- The rider in front of you does not need to turn around and look at you as he backs, in fact the exercise will work better if he keeps his focus forward and uses one hand to swing the stick – this way you will both stay straight.
- Staying straight is a key to success in this exercise, it will keep you in a safe position. If you allow your horse to turn his nose away from the tail in front, you will be in a position to be kicked.

Troubleshooting
- *My horse keeps getting close to the horse in front!*
  Pat Parelli has a great saying in these situations: "I've never seen it take longer than two days." Hang in there, keep doing what you're doing and be effective. Before long, your horse will figure out what happens before what *happens* happens.

55. Swing The Energy

Prerequisites
- A willing buddy partner.
- Safety while riding.

Outcomes
- Improve your horse's attention on your body language and begin to slow and speed up his gait off just your energy.
- Cause it to be more effort to be near his buddy and allow him to have more relaxation when away from his buddy.

Steps

1. As you are riding with your buddy, ask your horse to lengthen his stride for 5 strides, don't pick up the next gait, just lengthen within the gait.

2. Ask your horse to shorten his stride within the gait for 5 steps.
3. Repeat. As you do this you will be getting closer and then farther away from your buddy. Focus on your horse lightly responding to you and what you are asking, so that he begins to respond from your energy.

4. When you have asked him to adjust his stride and he is a little distance from his buddy, allow him to carry on in his natural gait. This will serve as the release/reward away from his buddy and create draw to the distance between you.

Savvy Tips
- You can do this exercise while riding FreeStyle on a casual rein or while riding on a concentrated rein in Finesse. If you choose to use a concentrated rein be sure your horse is responding to your seat and energy and not to just a pull on the reins.
- As you advance you can even build these transitions within gait towards passage if you choose!

Troubleshooting
- *My horse is not going forward off my energy, not even off my leg!*
Remember to go through your Phases:
  1. Smile.
  2. Squeeze.
  3. "Smooch" if you please.
  4. Spank.

Be sure to release your legs the moment he goes forward, the release is often more important than the pressure. If you follow these steps, your horse should begin to respond at a lighter and lighter Phase. Remember to give him the opportunity to be light by starting at Phase 1.

56. Rock Weight Front To Back By Buddy

Prerequisites
- Level 3 riding skills.
- A willing buddy and rider.

Outcomes
- Refining your communication with your horse so that you are able to just rock the weight without moving the feet.
- Giving your horse a task while he is with his buddy and taking him away to allow him to rest.

Steps

1. While you are with your buddy, pick up a soft touch/soft feel on your horse and wait until they are confident.
2. Using your body, ask your horse to rock his weight to the right, this might start with Sideways to the right.

3. Now move your horse Sideways to the left. Continue this pattern until you are able to move just enough to rock

your horse's weight without moving his feet.

4. Once your horse is responding with willingness and you feel a step of just weight rocking, ask your horse to walk away from his buddy and have a rest.

Savvy Tips

- This is a great exercise to play when your buddy is standing still. They don't have to do anything different and you can cause it to be more comfortable for your horse to stand away from his buddy.
- You can do this exercise for as long as you like and rotate between Sideways and weight rocking to keep it interesting for your horse.

Troubleshooting

- *My horse keeps drifting forwards when I ask for Sideways.*
  You can balance this by finishing each step Sideways with 2-3 steps backwards, which helps balance out your horse.
- *My horse tries to go back to his buddy as soon as I drop the reins to allow him rest.*
  Try not taking him as far away and see if he is able to stop his feet only a few feet from his buddy, then build up from there. Also, if your horse wants/needs to go back to his buddy, allow him to but then cause him to move his feet while he is next to his buddy. When you are ready to allow his feet to stop, go some distance from the buddy and try to stop there.

"I've never seen it take longer than two days."

57. Lollipop

Prerequisites
- Level 2 riding skills.
- A willing and safe buddy horse.

Outcomes
- Improving circles to the point that you only have 0-4 corrections with your reins per circle.
- Developing a pattern where your horse is welcome to stay with his buddy while he moves his feet, or he can drift away from his buddy and find relaxation and rest.

Steps

1. This exercise can be done while your buddy is in motion or standing still. You will start beside your buddy and ask your horse to circle his buddy.
2. You can add in transitions as you go, between walk and trot, even canter.
3. You can change direction while circling your buddy.

4. When your horse is more focused on you, offer him a chance to rest a few feet to the outside of the circle you were making. If your buddy is in motion, then your rest will be a relative distance from your buddy horse while you keep traveling forward with them.

Savvy Tips

- Be sure to circle your buddy horse at a safe distance so that you are far enough away that you do not get kicked and your horse does not try to kick the buddy horse.
- As your horse gets the hang of this game and the rest is away from his buddy, you can increase the size of the circle and add in more variations.

Troubleshooting

- *My horse keeps pushing in towards his buddy.*

  This is to be expected before your horse figures out the new pattern of where to find rest (away from his buddy). If he pushes in towards his buddy, ask him to go Sideways a few steps away from his buddy, then ask for the circle again. This will help your horse figure out the puzzle because going Sideways is harder work than walking a forwards circle.

58. Backwards Circle

Prerequisites
- Level 2 riding skills.
- A willing buddy horse and rider.

Outcomes
- Teach your horse to maintain gait backwards, so that he continues to go backwards by just following your energy and intention.
- Rewarding your horse for a light response or extra effort by allowing him to rest away from his buddy.
- This will help improve his athleticism and your communication.

Steps

1. This is a similar idea to the previous exercise, except now you will be asking your horse to back a circle. Start by asking your horse to back using the 9-Step Back up.

2. After your horse begins backing, use your leg to shift his HQ to keep him in a circle.

3. As long as you are a safe distance from your buddy horse you can change direction backwards through your circle.

4. When your horse is backing smoothly and responsively, ask him to yield his FQ away from his buddy and allow him to rest. As you increase the distance, you will ask him to walk off after you yield the FQ away and rest a little distance away from his buddy.

Savvy Tips

- As you back remember to have a strong focus, this will influence your horse more than your reins or legs.
- If your horse is having trouble moving off your leg while backing, you can stop backing, isolate yield the HQ (indirect rein) until he is back in position, then back again.
- Remember the nine steps of the 9-Step Back up:
  1. Lift the reins with one hand.
  2. Slide your other hand down both reins all the way to the neck.
  3. Separate your reins, one in each hand, fingers pointed forward.
  4. Close your pointer finger.
  5. Close your middle finger.
  6. Close your ring finger.
  7. Close your pinky finger.
  8. Bring your elbows back to your sides.
  9. Bring your belly button back towards your horse's tail with your elbows still by your side.

Troubleshooting

- *My horse was backing but now refuses to go back another step.*
  To unlock his feet you can use some indirect rein, just ask for a step at a time. When you ask for backwards again, reward each try with a little release.

59. Circle Splits

Prerequisites
- Both you and your buddy horse need to be working in Level 2 riding skills to make this successful.
- A stump/barrel/cone and space to ride around it.

Outcomes
- Improve your circles at the same time your buddy horse improves theirs.
- Timing your rewards so that you both go in different directions to give your horses rest.
- Using this exercise to balance your horse's tendency to drop into the circle or to veer outside the circle.

Steps

1. This is a great exercise to help improve your circles as well as increasing draw away from the herd. Start by circling a stump/barrel/cone with your buddy.
2. You can circle at whatever speed you like and include transitions. You can also circle at a different speed than your buddy to add variety as you play.
3. When both of your horses are responding nicely, take your horse a few feet away from the circle and allow him to stop.

4. At the same time your buddy can take their horse to the stump to rest.

Savvy Tips

- You can alternate who stops at the stump and who stops outside the circle. The best way to pick who stops where is based on the horse's natural tendencies. If your horse wants to cut into the center of the circle then stopping him on the outside will help. If your horse wants to drift to the outside of the circle then stopping him in the center will help balance him out.
- You can do this exercise out on the trail if you come to a clearing and your horse needs to move his feet.
- As you advance, you can also add variety to this exercise by going in a different direction than your buddy on the circle.

Troubleshooting

- *My horse is going faster than I want on the circle.*
  You can bring your circle in closer to the object you are circling. The smaller the circle, the harder it will be for your horse to run off. As your horse gains impulsion and can control himself you can increase the size of your circle again.

60. Sideways Away

Prerequisites
- Level 2+ riding skills.
- A willing buddy horse.

Outcomes
- Use Sideways as a tool to show your horse that going away from his buddy is where he finds rest and relaxation.
- Improve Sideways and start getting Sideways off just your intention.
- Improving your speed while going Sideways, so that you can build towards trotting Sideways.

Steps

1. While with your buddy, ask your horse to go Sideways away from his buddy.

2. Ask him to go Sideways towards his buddy.
3. Go Sideways so far this way that you pass your buddy. When you get a few feet away, allow your horse to stop

and pause for a moment, then go back towards your buddy. Repeat this process 5-7 times.

4. When your horse is feeling connected and responsive, ask him to go Sideways away and allow him to rest for a long time away from his buddy.

Savvy Tips
- As your horse figures out this puzzle you can increase the distance you ask your horse to go Sideways away from his buddy. You can even start to play a point to point Sideways past your buddy to help increase draw away.
- Keep in mind the dynamics of Sideways: Focus where you want to go as you ask your horse for Sideways; open the door with your leg in the direction you are going and "push" with the opposite leg to cause your horse to go Sideways.

Troubleshooting
- *My horse is so heavy on my leg, I'm getting a cramp asking him to go Sideways.*
  You may need to use some rhythmic pressure to support the Porcupine off your leg. You can use your mecate, Carrot Stick, or saddle strings. While asking for Sideways and using your leg, add rhythmic pressure by tapping your leg first and then tapping whichever Zone of your horse isn't moving.

61. "Sideways Wars"

Prerequisites
- Level 2+ riding skills for you and your buddy.
- Buddy horse rider needs to have a Carrot Stick and be confident to swing it while riding.

Outcomes
- Faster and lighter Sideways by using your buddy to provide motivation.
- Allowing you to offer the suggestion and your buddy to be the reason why your horse should follow your suggestion.
- Another situation you can provide rest away from your horse's buddy.

Steps
1. Fun! With a willing buddy horse rider using a Carrot Stick, you can play Sideways Wars. For this game your buddy will ask his horse to walk towards you while he swings his Carrot Stick.

2. As your buddy comes towards you, you will ask your horse to go Sideways away from the buddy.
3. You will set up the suggestion for your horse, your buddy will add pressure (if needed) to motivate your horse to move. (It's like playing bull fighter!)
4. After your horse willingly yields Sideways away from his

buddy allow him to rest away, then play again going the other way.

Savvy Tips

- This will help improve not only your horse's draw away from his buddy, but also his Sideways and lightness of response to your request.
- You can also carry a Carrot Stick and play this game back with your buddy horse and rider, this way they can have fun too.
- If your buddy horse is not ridable yet, you can do this exercise with the buddy horse's human on the ground, using the same technique.

Troubleshooting

- *My horse gets scared and wants to run away as his buddy approaches him.*

  Your horse may need a little more space. See if your buddy horse can start 12-22 feet away, this may help your horse to not feel so pressured.

"You have to be effective to be understood,
and understood to be effective."

62. Rider Squeeze

Prerequisites
- A willing buddy horse and rider.
- Level 2 riding skills.

Outcomes
- Improving your horse's confidence in following your leadership in tight spaces.
- Creating flow between you and your buddy where your horse finds rest when he is away from his buddy.

Steps

1. For this exercise you will be playing Squeeze Game just as you would on the ground. Only your buddy and their horse will take the position you would be in if you were on the ground, and you and your horse will take the position of the horse.
2. Once you are both in position, ask your horse to walk through the Squeeze.

3. Turn on the other side, be sure to disengage while Zone 1 stays aimed towards your buddy (just as your horse would

if your buddy was the one sending them through). Wait for 7 seconds and then repeat in the opposite direction.

4. After you practice this a few times you can start going further and further before turning to face your buddy. This will help your horse play approach and retreat with his buddy and get rewarded for going away from his buddy.

Savvy Tips
- Be sure your buddy gives you enough space in the Squeeze so that your horse doesn't feel pressured to rush through the space or get defensive.
- As you improve and your horse gets accustomed to this exercise, you can increase the distance to 45 feet or more before you turn and face.

Troubleshooting
- *My horse is rushing through the Squeeze.*
  Ask your buddy to back up 10 feet or more to give your horse more room. Also, your horse may be feeling unsure about the Squeeze you are asking him to do. In this case, as long as you feel safe, keep doing the pattern and turn him to face the Squeeze as soon as you go through until he gains confidence, then stop there. If you feel unsafe, this may be a good time to get off and send your horse through the Squeeze on the ground until he feels confident.

63. Pairs Dance

Prerequisites
• Both you and your buddy horse need Level 2+ riding savvy.

Outcomes
• Flow, rhythm, and timing. By giving yourself something to focus on (like staying next to your buddy), it can help you find flow with your horse. Also, when you are ready to rest, it continues the pattern of allowing your horse to rest away from his buddy.

Steps
1. You will work with your buddy for this exercise. If you feel safe with your horses a few feet from each other you can use a Savvy String as part of the dance. Each of you will hold one end of the string while you ride.

2. As you ride play with Sideways, transitions, and Circles, all while holding the savvy string.
3. Of course if things get too lively you can simply let go of the string at any time to stay safe.

4. After you have played for 5-7 minutes, allow the string to drop out of one of your hands and ride your horses apart to allow them to rest.

Savvy Tips

- By riding together and including things that might be challenging for your horse, then allowing him to move away from his buddy to rest, you are helping him realize that comfort is wherever you are asking him to go.
- Include things that you can have fun with and remember, if your horses get in a position where they want to kick at each other, yield the HQ away by turning their nose towards the other horse – this will swing the kicking HQ away and give you a chance to get out of the situation.
- Be very mindful of your string and be sure it doesn't end up under your horse's tail or your buddy horse's tail – this can really bother horses, particularly if you haven't prepared for it yet.

Troubleshooting

- *My horse is feeling a lot of pressure being this close to his buddy.*
In this situation you may need to give your horse a little more space. You can do this by forgetting about the Savvy String all together, or you can tie two savvy strings together and see if the extra distance helps your horse.

Well Done Completing The Riding Section!

You have taken huge steps in improving your relationship with your horse and building a partnership your horse is glad to be a part of! You should see the improvement and your horse's desire to be with you.

As A Reminder Of Where To Go From Here

Now that you have completed at least one of the ground sections and the riding section exercises, you may find it useful to use additional sections and adjust the exercises to fit your situation. These sections will review some of the information you just covered and they will give you additional tools and perspectives for continuing to build your relationship.

The last step is to read over the Emergency Strategy section so that you will be better prepared for unforeseen situations if they arise.

Also, at any time you feel you need a little "refresher," have a quick read back over the theory section as a reminder to look at things from your horse's perspective.

SECTION 5

Emergency Strategies & Exercises

This section is focused on strategies,
exercises, and reminders to help you deal with herd
bound issues – in the moment.
After you have done the prior and
proper preparation at home, there will still be times
your horse becomes attached to another horse.
This section will focus on
what to do when this happens.

Horsenality Filter: Emergency Strategies

As you progress through the following section you may find the Horsenality filter below useful to help tailor each exercise to fit your individual horse.

LB Extrovert

- Be aware that you have to be more interesting than everything else!
- Be active, move his feet.
- If you are arguing with him, you are on the wrong track – put him away and cool off.

RB Extrovert

- Do more 180 degree turns more often.
- Do not block Zone 1 – direct it.
- He needs your leadership to help him calm down.

LB Introvert

- Play mental games, get him thinking.
- Remember to not pick a fight with someone bigger than you.
- Become more interesting – use your energy up and DOWN, use interesting Phases.
- Add variety.

RB Introvert

- Ask less, reward the slightest relaxation (smoother breathing counts).
- Be aware of his subtle signs of stress so that he doesn't have to get to the "blow up" stage.
- Be subtle but clear.
- PATTERNS, and time to relax, are key.

Safety Reminders

Your safety is Number 1. If you get hurt then you can't be there for your horse. Be safe first, then proceed.

Rewards Away From The Buddy

Rest, scratches, food, water/molasses water, grass, rolling.

Distance Away From Buddy For Reward

12 feet, 15 feet, 22 feet, 32 feet, 45 feet, etc.

Level Recommendations

Adjust the exercise to fit your savvy level: Level 1 – 12-foot line; Level 2 – 22-foot line, Level 3-4 – 45-foot line.

"Be as light as possible,
and as firm as necessary."

64. Trailering Challenges

Savvy Tips

- If you are having trouble loading him to get to the clinic/show/trail or to go home, sometimes the simple tip of pointing the nose of the truck in the direction the horse wants to go can be enough to encourage him to go forward into the trailer.

- If your horse has loaded but is worried in the trailer, sometimes just getting on the road will help this horse settle. If you know your horse may get worried after he is on the trailer, have all of your things ready to go, so that after he has loaded you can pull out ASAP.

- If your horse is scared and right-brained about getting in the trailer, be sure to send him in, don't lead him in – they are right-brain and could run over you. After the horse is in (most trailers), it will be safer to close the doors before tying your horse. This will prevent him from leaning back on the halter and possibly slipping or breaking the tie while the doors are still open. After you arrive at your destination, remember to untie him before opening the doors, this way if he is in a hurry to get out he won't have the opportunity to pull back on the halter. Last, for this horse you can load with a buddy horse whenever possible, this will help give him confidence in the herd.

65. At The Clinic

Savvy Tips

• If you notice your horse is worried and the clinic has not yet begun, you have the opportunity to play approach and retreat with the new stall/buddy/safety. Think of the same strategies you have prepared with at home, now you are building your horse's confidence with you in this new environment.

• If during the clinic your horse is worried about where his buddy horse is, see if your friend can move the buddy horse close to yours. Now that you are in a new area and particularly after a trailer ride, you may need to rebuild the patterns you had in place at home. If you have done the prep work it should take much less time this time. As the clinic progresses, work on getting your horses more confident being separated again, playing while they are close and allowing them to rest while they are separate.

"Prior and Proper Preparation,
Prevents 'P'-Poor Performance."

66. My Horse Is Worried In The Stall

Strategies

- Sometimes the biggest thing we can do to help our horse is to hurry up and relax. It may be best for your horse to leave him in the stall (your stressed energy is most likely making things worse for your horse). Be sure he is safe and then walk away, relax, and focus on the things you need to get done.

- If you are worried about your horse's safety and your horse trailered in with another, or is buddies with another horse at the facility, see if a friend can move that horse close to yours. Ideally you could keep some stalls between your horse and his buddy, this will serve you later, but if the only thing that will help you and your horse is to put him next to his buddy then do this. You can always work on separating them in a few hours when things have calmed down.

- Another option for if your horse is worried about the stall itself, play approach and retreat with the stall until he gains confidence and is able to stand confidently.

- With an extrovert, you may need to take him out of the stall and play with him intensely so that he is ready to stand still in the stall. This will take some savvy and quick thinking on your part, so you can be the judge of whether you are ready to use this strategy or not.

67. My Horse Is Scared In The Arena

Strategies

- Use the Horsenality filter to get them focused on you. You may need to give him more time and honor his thresholds if he is introverted. You may need to find patterns for him to move his feet in, if he is more extroverted.

- You have to be more interesting and comfortable than everything else. By getting your horse to focus on you and trust in your leadership, he will become less focused and worried about the arena being scary.

- Smile and say "You are being an excellent prey animal!" This simple change in our attitude can go a long way in helping our horses.

- Ask for help from the Instructor. When things are more than you feel able to handle, you can go to the Instructor and ask for help. After all, that is why we sign up for courses with Instructors – to get their help!

68. My Horse Is Attached To The Horse He Trailered In With

Strategies

• Pretend you are starting again at home and practice the exercises by your buddy and rest away from them. This should take less time now that you have built a strong pattern at home. By taking the time it takes at home you have established a stronger relationship and more trust and respect from your horse. This will carry over to the new situation and it should take less time to get your horse refocused on you.

• Another option that can help in certain situations is to stall them away from each other if possible. This way your horse doesn't rest and eat next to his buddy for 18 hours and then get pulled away to "work."

• Leave the arena at the same time so you don't stress your horse. Often the strategies that seem the most logical to us actually don't help our relationship with our horse. After you have finished a great session with your horse, or any kind of session, the last thing you want to do is get him stressed when he sees his buddy leaving the arena, then take him to his buddy to rest, eat and relax after he spent a stress-filled time with you. Simply set this situation up so that you can leave at the same time, at this stage you might not want to start an additional training session.

69. My Horse Is Attached To Someone Or Something Still In The Barn

Strategies

• You can choose to be more interesting and important than whatever is in the barn that your horse is attached to. This can take a LOT of savvy and you may need to "channel" Pat Parelli to help you with this! Basically you have to match your horse's energy plus 4-ounces and be 1-3 steps ahead of him at all times. Once you can get his attention on you and he begins to calm down he will come off of adrenaline and things will begin to slow down... Until his buddy whinnies again, then be ready to go again!

• Another option, if you think he might be worried and the clinic/show has not yet begun. You can stay up late and/ or get up early to invest some time in playing approach and retreat with whatever he is attached to/afraid of. The best strategies for this will be in the previous sections of the book (find the section that most currently matches his conditions and "work" your way through those exercises).

• In the end you want your horse to see you as the leader. This is what will help him the most in new situations because you will be his leader and make up half of his herd of two.

"Put the Relationship FIRST."

70. My Horse Has Druthers Towards His Buddy/Food/Stall/People/etc.

Strategies

• Keep in mind everything you have learned throughout this book. If your horse is telling you he would rather be somewhere else as opposed to where he is, it is your job to help him see why it is more desirable to be where you are suggesting. Use the strategies mentioned previously in the book; if your horse has strong druthers you will most likely have to use these strategies on a daily basis to help your horse create new patterns.

71. Challenges in Class While The Group is Gathered

Savvy Tips

• The biggest tip to helping your horse find 'stand still' in the group is getting them in the mood to hold still. If you have an extroverted horse this may mean he needs you to play a lot before the clinic/horse show so that he is ready to keep his feet still.

• As your horse progresses through the clinic he will most likely soon realize that the horseshoe is a comfortable place to be where he can rest with no "pressure." Until then, hang in there and see if some of the following exercises help.

• Also, if you are at a clinic or lesson, keep in mind that you are there to improve your horsemanship. When things feel like they are beyond your scope to handle, ask the Instructor for help. That is what they are there for and most likely why you have signed up for the event.

72. Use Your Buddy!

Prerequisites
- A willing and able buddy horse.
- Time before the event begins.

Outcomes
- Take your horse's idea of being with his buddy and use it to help you build his confidence in the new area.
- Finish by allowing your horse to find relaxation and rest in the new environment and away from his buddy.

Steps
1. Now that your horse is worried about the arena you can use your horse's buddy to help!

2. If your horse's buddy is confident in the arena, use this draw to your advantage. Move your horse's feet outside of the arena (you can use any of the patterns previously mentioned in the book).

3. Bring your horse into the arena or if he is really worried, just close to the arena with Zone 1 facing the arena, and allow him to rest.

4. If he feels the need to move his feet again, take him outside the arena and move his feet, then take him back to the arena and allow him to rest.

Savvy Tips

• As you play with this exercise it is better if you allow your horse to rest in the arena with his buddy but not right next to his buddy. You are trying to use the buddy horse as draw without creating the mother-foal bond between them.

• If you notice that your horse is worried about the arena the night before, it will give you the option to play with this several times before the event begins.

Troubleshooting

• *My horse wants to roll in the sand.*

As long as it is allowed at the arena you are in, allow him to roll! This is a great sign that he is coming off adrenaline and realizes how itchy he is and how good it would feel to scratch off in the sand!

*"Turn your frustrations
into your fascinations."*

73. Scared Of The Arena Edges

Prerequisites

• Level 1 ground skills.

Outcomes

• Use Sideways to move your horse's feet and allow the natural tendency to go forward in Sideways help your horse get more confident with the arena edges.

• Encourage your horse's idea to move his feet. Allow it to be his idea to become curious about what he was afraid of.

Steps

1. Often the first thing predators want to do when their horses are afraid of something is to take them to it. Let's do somewhat of the opposite: Ask your horse to go Sideways around the arena.

2. Allow him to stay away from the rail at whatever distance he likes, your job is to ask for Sideways. If he offers to go closer to the rail you can allow him to rest for a moment.

3. Send him in a half-circle around you and go Sideways in the other direction.

4. You can continue this pattern, each time your horse offers to get closer to the rail allow him to get curious and check things out in his own time. If he needs to move his feet again, offer Sideways and repeat.

Savvy Tips

• Keep your feet traveling in a rhythm and on a straight line, if your horse drifts away from you let your string out so that "you" can still touch him.

Troubleshooting

• *My horse went straight to the rail.*

Perfect! Problem solved, move on.

74. Half Circles At The Wall On The Ground

Prerequisites

• A wall that your horse will not jump/push through.

• A willing Instructor.

Outcomes

• Understand that your horse needs to move his feet and give him a pattern that helps him think.

• Continue moving his feet until it is his idea to relax.

• You make the suggestion and allow your horse to find the answer.

Steps

1. Once you are positioned at the end of the horseshoe and near a wall, place your rear end on the wall.

2. Ask your horse to go around you in a circle, of course the wall will interrupt his circle and only allow for a half circle. If he offers to stop, allow it.

3. If he chooses to keep going, encourage his idea and just allow the wall to help interrupt his pattern of racing forwards.

4. Allow him as much time as he needs, your job is to protect your personal space and listen to the Instructor. When your horse offers a stand still, allow it.

Savvy Tips

- There are times when we do not have the skills or knowledge to help our horse come off adrenaline. But half circles/180 degree turns help horses come back to using their brains and come off adrenaline. So, you can use a wall instead of doing figure 8 or changes of direction to help your horse.

- It's important for many Horsenalities to not be blocked in Zone 1 when situations like this arise. If an extrovert feels blocked when he wants to go forward he is likely to become more "disobedient" and harder to manage. It is important to give him a pattern where he can burn off some of that adrenaline.

Troubleshooting

- *I don't feel safe.*

  Ask for help from the Instructor and/or put your horse away until you can get help.

75. Box Step While Riding

Prerequisites
• Level 2+ riding skills.

Outcomes
• Give your horse a pattern when he needs to move his feet while you stay focused on your goal.

• Helping your horse find the comfort of holding his feet still.

• Having a relaxed and quiet horse while standing still.

Steps
1. Pick up a soft feel with your horse and ask for one step Sideways.

2. Then ask for one step backwards.

3. Then ask for one step Sideways the other way.

4. Last, ask for one step forwards and repeat this process (you will be making a little box), until they offer to hold still.

Savvy Tips
• This is a great thing to do with your horse while still keeping your attention on the Instructor. It allows you to keep your focus up, stay in your spot in the lineup and allows your horse to move his feet.

• Keep your focus forward on the Instructor and continue listening to the group discussion while allowing the box step to become a smooth dance until your horse chooses to keep his feet still.

Troubleshooting

• *My horse is not getting any better, he is wanting to move more and I am feeling unsafe.*

This may be a great time to get off and get individual help from the Instructor. Or, if that is not an option, you may choose to take your horse away from the group a little ways and offer him some productive ways to move his feet. Such as, Figure 8 and Circles with changes of direction.

76. To And Fro While Riding

Prerequisites

• Level 2+ riding skills.

Outcomes

• Give your horse a pattern when he needs to move his feet while you stay focused on your goal.

• Helping your horse find the comfort of holding his feet still.

• Having a relaxed and quiet horse while standing still.

Steps

1. While in the horseshoe you can usually do this exercise without anyone getting distracted from the Instructor. Start with a soft touch or soft feel with your horse.

2. Ask for 1-2 steps backwards, give a moment reward.

3. Ask for 1-2 steps forwards, give a moment reward (just a moment and not longer because if you are trying this it is because your horse is not yet ready to keep his feet still).

4. Continue this pattern until your horse seems like he might want to keep his feet still, then offer a loose rein to check. You can always repeat if he is not yet ready. Also, you can refine this until your horse is just rocking his weight back and forth without moving his feet.

Savvy Tips

• Be sure you aren't backing your horse with your reins. You want your horse to be responsive off your seat first, the reins only come into effect if he doesn't respond.

• Keep in mind that your goal is for your horse to want to keep his feet still, so if he offers to stop them, reward him. If he needs to move them more, help him by continuing to give him positive patterns to move his feet on.

Troubleshooting

• *My horse is getting worse.*

You may need to go ahead and get off and/or ask the Instructor for help.

77. Swaying In The "Breeze" While Riding

Prerequisites

• Level 2+ riding skills.

Outcomes

• Give your horse a pattern when he needs to move his feet while you stay focused on your goal.

• Helping your horse find the comfort of holding his feet still.

• Having a relaxed and quiet horse while standing still.

Steps

1. Pick up a soft touch/feel on your horse.

2. Ask for a step or two Sideways. Pause.

3. Ask for a step or two Sideways in the other direction. Pause. Repeat.

4. Continue this "swaying" back and forth until your horse offers to keep his feet still. When he does, give him a big reward. At the same time be ready to ask for a positive pattern of feet moving again, very soon.

Savvy Tips

• As you are asking your horse to go Sideways, keep in mind your Phases: You don't want to get stuck at a high Phase. Each time your horse responds, start back at Phase 1 asking for the next movement, even if it's another step in the same direction.

• If at any time it feels like your horse is gaining energy and/or you feel unsafe, go ahead and get off. You can always get back on.

Troubleshooting

• *My horse is going Sideways back and forth on their own and I am just sitting here doing nothing!*

Smart horse! Now you can change the pattern to Yo-Yo or box step. Each time your horse takes over (or ideally right before they take over), change the pattern. This should help keep their brain engaged and help to keep them focused on your leadership.

Congratulations! You Have Completed This Program. Well done!

By now you should be feeling that your hard work and diligence has paid off. You have a horse who is more excited to see you and willing to spend time with you. They may even be choosing you over the other horses!

If you still want more from your relationship with your horse, I highly recommend continuing through the Parelli program and growing your relationship; accomplishing amazing things with your horse!

Again, well done for taking a step in making your horse's world a better place and thank you for being part of the Parelli mission: *"To make the world a better place for horses and humans."*

SECTION 6

Pattern Progress Pages

Pattern Progress Pages

Refer to the Theory guide section "Creating a Pattern" to plan your program.

Week 1

Date Week 1 started: _____

Date Week 1 finished: _____

Week 2

Date Week 2 started: _____

Date Week 2 finished: _____

Weeks 3-5

Date Weeks 3-5 started: _____

Date Weeks 3-5 finished: _____

Pattern Progress Pages

Refer to the Theory guide section "Creating a Pattern" to plan your program.

Week 1

Date Week 1 started: _____

Date Week 1 finished: _____

Week 2

Date Week 2 started: _____

Date Week 2 finished: _____

Weeks 3-5

Date Weeks 3-5 started: _____

Date Weeks 3-5 finished: _____

Pattern Progress Pages

Refer to the Theory guide section "Creating a Pattern" to plan your program.

Week 1

·						

Date Week 1 started: _____

Date Week 1 finished: _____

Week 2

Date Week 2 started: _____

Date Week 2 finished: _____

Weeks 3-5

Date Weeks 3-5 started: _____

Date Weeks 3-5 finished: _____

we have to out fumble our
   horses ... drop rope,
stick ... all other fumbles –
don't stop – keep going   the
horse probably won't even
notice

separate our energy from our
emotions

take care of the small things
friendly but <u>clear boundries</u>

break things down smaller + smaller

spend lots of down time with your horse
enjoyable time for them
              understand the
DNA – <u>need</u> to be with the herd

Be ~~present~~ present with a plan